Harriet L. Adams

A Woman's Journeyings in the New Northwest

Harriet L. Adams

A Woman's Journeyings in the New Northwest

ISBN/EAN: 9783744761901

Printed in Europe, USA, Canada, Australia, Japan

Cover: Foto ©Andreas Hilbeck / pixelio.de

More available books at **www.hansebooks.com**

A WOMAN'S JOURNEYINGS

IN THE

NEW NORTHWEST.

BY

HARRIET L. ADAMS.

CLEVELAND, OHIO:
B-P PRINTING CO.,
1892.

TO

All the Women,

Whether inside or outside the realm of White Ribbon, who bore a part of my burdens and cheered me on my way,

These "Journeyings" are lovingly dedicated.

H. L. A.

PREFACE.

In placing this simple and hastily written account of personal experience before the public, I wish to say that I am not unmindful of the fact that the haps and mishaps falling to the lot of an individual are not supposed to possess a high degree of interest for the world at large; but having read many scholarly dissertations on the West, and ostensibly graphic descriptions of Western life, without having received other than a vague impression much of which was erroneous and quickly vanished upon personal observation, I have taken the liberty of presuming that there are others under like impressions, and that to such, a plain statement of actual occurrences, while possessing no great merit, may be helpful in some small particular. As a consequence, I have endeavored to narrate lucidly what I saw, what I heard and the impressions I received; which has necessitated a relation of what I did, and what I said. If the reader thinks the writer is given too much prominence, I beg his or her forbearance, on the plea that where one is both actor and chronicler, self cannot well be ignored.

With these few words of explanation, and the sincere wish that the following pages may bring something of information or amusement to all to whose notice they come, I submit them to the mercy of the reading public, of which I have no reason to complain, without further remarks.

HARRIET L. ADAMS.

Cleveland, Ohio.

CHAPTER I.—A wide awake face—An important conductor—The Bad Lands—Chinamen's camp—Rocky building lots.

CHAPTER II.—Cheney's lakes—Awakened by Indians—Afraid of lightning—Indians celebrate the Fourth—Buying a "cayuse."

CHAPTER III.—Egypt—A balking team—Entrance to Coulee City—Western horsewomanship—Stock raising by women.

CHAPTER IV.—Spokane Falls—Hillside wheatfields—Misleading names—How I went to Pine City—Medical Lake—Weary overlanders.

CHAPTER V.—Yews and ferns—Beauties of Puget Sound—A rainbow—On the Straits of San Juan de Fuca—Picking blackberries late in October—The "Infidel Colony."

CHAPTER VI.—A night ride on Lopez Island—Tons of strawberries—A unique concert—Aground in an open boat—La Conner—"No Bar Hotel."

CHAPTER VII.—Taking up, and holding down, a claim—"The Devil's Bread Pan"—Mud—Port Townsend—Something of a storm.

CHAPTER VIII —Hotel de Haro—Everybody go aft—Clams—The long suffering cow—Seattle Y. M. C. A.—Olympia's why's.

CHAPTER IX.—Portland's novel feature—Willamette Valley—"Webfeet" and "Mossbacks"—Early settlers—Landslides.

CHAPTER X.—Chill, damp misery—Climbing heights and fathoming depths—Elkton's gem—My first sight of the Pacific Ocean—Going to the Coquille River—Ashland.

CHAPTER XI.—An Indian woman and the U. P. R. R. Co.—Climbing the heights at Bridal Veil Falls—The Dalles—Experience at Grants—Visit to a jail.

CHAPTER XII.—Sage brush—Mountain Home rabbits—A town on wheels—Attending a Mormon meeting—Some remarks on Mormonism.

CHAPTER XIII.—Where the women vote—Hilda—The Ames Monument—Some ministers—Not an equal equality

CHAPTER XIV.—Last scenes of the panorama—Nebraska drouths—Intelligent women—Omaha—Over nine thousand miles—Thanks.

CHAPTER I.

Having long purposed making a trip to that much "boomed" but at that time by me untraversed country known by the various titles, "The West," "The Coast" and the "Pacific Slope," on Monday, May 5th, 1890, I took a west-bound train on the Lake Shore and Michigan Southern R. R., from Cleveland, Ohio, with no particular objective point except a cabin on a bunch-grass ranch in Eastern Washington, where I expected to make a short visit, but feeling fully equipped for my journeyings in the possession of a talisman in the form of a letter of introduction and commendation from Miss Frances E. Willard, president of the National Woman's Christian Temperance Union, who had, also, kindly opened the way for me by sending before me word of my coming.

The freshness of the May verdure as seen from the car window between Cleveland and Chicago was soothing to nerves long suffering from overwork and worry, but full familiarity with the scenery of the route rendered it without other interest. I arrived in the latter city about nine o'clock the same night, and as my route was over the Northern Pacific R. R., the eastern terminus of which is reached at St. Paul by way of the Wisconsin Central, from Chicago, I was hastening towards a transfer carriage for the latter road under the triple burden of traveling bag, lunch basket and rug-strap bundle when a clear, strong voice pronounced my name but a few feet distant.

As the thought of a telegram flitted through my brain, I turned in the direction from whence the voice had come, and answered at random to the wilderness of moving forms, "That's me."

Immediately a wide awake face was thrust through the swaying mass of heads, and the same voice that had uttered the name said: "Mr. Campbell wired me from Cleveland, and I'm to see you to your sleeper at the Wisconsin Central Depot."

Then I began to see clearly. Mr. Tom D. Campbell, the district passenger agent stationed at Cleveland for the Northern Pacific R. R. had agreed to telegraph for sleeping car accommodations and had assured me that all proper courtesies would be extended by the officials of the Wisconsin Central; but I had not expected to meet with such a helpful reception at the outset.

A fuller solution of the matter came out, however, when my escort added, "I understand you are a W. C. T. U. woman, and although we look after all our passengers, I was determined not to miss you."

As we were being driven over to the Wisconsin Central Depot the young man told me of his efforts to break the liquor fiend's bonds, by which he had himself been held—how he had twice thrown them off, and as many times taken them on again, but at last, by force of will and constant activity of body and mind in proper channels, had then held the habit of drink back for more than a year.

"You will understand," said he, "why I take such an interest in the temperance women's work."

And when I thought of the national, state and municipal governments all combined in proffering the cup to the young man's lips; and strong manhood wistfully grasping the hand of woman for aid in the endeavor to withstand such temptation, I could only wonder why woman was not made the stronger instead of the weaker vessel.

Eleven o'clock saw me at rest in a comfortable "sleeper" speeding away towards St. Paul. The night was cool, but Tuesday morning came in bright and clear, and as I sat in our cozy car, with the sunny view outside, and the happy notes of two canaries, owned by fellow travelers, inside, the long journey of over two thousand miles lying between me and my first stopping point, lost its aspect of weariness. The only inharmonious occurrence of the day was the visit of a conductor who took charge of the train at one point. That official entered our car (and the others also, as I afterwards learned,) seemingly entertaining the idea that the people before him were all possessed of brains of inferior calibre or blighted activity, the emanations from which should be looked upon by him with a superior and unswerving disdain. As might have been expected, considering the intelligence of the traveling public of America, he met with some obstacles. From where I sat I could see women's faces flush as he spoke to them, and simple looking countrymen cower before his all-sufficient manner. Remembering it was said that a bear would, often, pass on harmlessly if one sat still and pointed something at it, I simply held forth my ticket in speechless suspense. But when he pocketed it and handed me in exchange a penciled card showing the limit for which my ticket had called reduced by two days, I felt compelled to ask if the card would hold good in case of delay.

"You have nothing to do with that. You have only to keep this card and show it when you are asked," said he, as he tapped the seat arm with his pencil and gazed up at the ceiling of the car.

Between a strong desire to laugh and the sense of a swift wave of heat sweeping up to my usually cool department of thought, I was dumb for a moment, but then managed to say civilly, "I only asked for information. The matter was talked over before starting, and the limit was made to avoid confusion in case of delay, I believe."

He then informed me that he paid no attention to ticket agents; that they had no right to issue such tickets; that he "knew his business" and did not intend to make an exception in one case among the "many thousands" he had to deal with.

And then—I arose, bodily from my seat and mentally to the occasion, and, endeavoring to observe the proprieties by holding my voice down to that pitch said to be "an excellent thing in a woman," and prefacing my remarks with the conventional "beg pardon," I told the man I believed I knew my rights, duties and privileges in the matter, and that unless he assured me I would have no trouble from his curtailment of the limit of my ticket, and apologized for his unseemly conduct, I would report him to his superiors from the first telegraph station.

Immediately such expressions as "Good!" "That's right!" coming from different parts of the car convinced me that I had gained the good will of my fellow travelers, whatever the final result might be.

I hardly expected to hear anything more from the conductor, and was preparing my telegram, when he returned and made full apology; in consideration of which I mention no names.

Night came on, Tuesday, soon after leaving Brainerd, Minn., and morning found us near Sanborn, N. D. The day was simply perfect, and the passengers amused themselves by watching for prairie dogs and rabbits, which were enjoying the sunshine. In fact, there was nothing else of interest for the eye to rest on; the entire distance to Bismarck showing nothing but gray, rolling prairie, with here and there deposits of pure alkali, and tiny and, often, abandoned cabins with long distances between. A few school-houses were among the latter, their location suggesting the idea that they had been dropped ready-made, from the sky, and at once explaining the sufferings of teachers and pupils in winter, of which Eastern people read so many accounts. One thing gave me a favorable impression regarding the humanity of the fearless pioneers who are endeavoring to bring those plains into blossom and bearing, and that is, they harness their oxen.

In the settlements where I saw oxen working, I observed that the heavy, irksome yoke had been done away with, breast straps and traces being substituted. The Department of Mercy of the W. C. T. U. may make a note of this.

Several hours west of Bismarck we came into scenery presenting such a startling contrast to that through which we had passed as to cause the most apathetic to gaze in wonder; and the question, "Could this ever have been done without hands?" asked by one passenger, was quickly answered by another with, "It is too stupendous to ever have been done by hands." The section of country into which we entered, and which is known as "The Bad Lands," is made up of detached hills of solid rock, many of them perfectly bare at the base and summit and with nothing but sparse grass patches covering the intermediate space. By some process of nature so far beyond the full grasp of the finite mind that the theories of geologists shed but little certain light upon it, these hills have been worn into most wonderful and artistic shapes. Rude models for churches, castles and cottages; for forts, ships, lighthouses and many other products of human mechanism are to be seen on every hand. The section is said to be rich in minerals, and the future millionaires who shall dig their fortunes in silver or gold out of those rocks can plan their domiciles from those patterns by the Great Architect of all.

Darkness overtook us at Glendive, Mont., and the early morning light showed us the smart town of Billings, in the same state. Soon the snow-capped peaks of the "Rockies" began to stand out through the blue haze in which they were enveloped, and eye-straining and exclamations were renewed. At a small station called Big Timber, where the train stopped about half an hour, the ground each side of the track was covered with yellow mountain daisies, and in a twinkling a hundred or more passengers were gathering boquets and taking in the exhilarating air with all the enjoyment of children in the "fresh air camps" of less pretensions. During the day, as the train wound in and out among the rocks and labored up steep inclines, it brought us now and then to little towns bright and soft with spring verdure—emerald gems set in granite, which had been produced by laborious irrigation, but were very restful to the overstrained eyes of sightseers. In truth, some of the cozy little homes wrought out and maintained in those rugged wilds through privation and effort not easily estimated by those fresh from Eastern comforts and facilities were inviting enough to tempt one to turn away from the more advanced civilization and find recompense in the humility taught by the mightiness of God's handiwork.

But there were, also, sights that repelled the finer senses. The blighting effects of alcohol and tobacco were everywhere present; and I was forced to wonder why men could not find sufficient vent for their destructive tendencies in razing those ruder of God's temples—the everlasting hills, without turning to rend the finer—their own bodies. As the train stopped at Elliston, a gentleman who had visited the town told me that of its thirty business places, eleven were saloons. Yet Elliston is not, nor are the Montana towns generally, worse than other places.

At Drummond, (Mont.,) we again sought our berths, awaking at Trout Creek station, in Idaho, to find an entire change in weather and vegetation. The scenery of dusty earth—except where irrigated—and clear sky had changed to fresh green foliage interspersed with flowers, and clouds that dripped so copiously as to create foaming rills and sadly interfere with the comfort of the lone miners camped on the mountain sides, who, with a trust that would be sublime did it not lead to such ludicrous predicaments, start out on prospecting tours provided with nothing but a blanket to interpose between their bodies and the granite beneath and heavens above. As we passed on through what is known as the "Cœur d'Alene country," which was at the height of a mining "boom" at the time, numbers of Chinamen, who are great surface miners, were to be seen grouped together in tents near the stations, and as they gazed disconsolately from under the dripping flaps, their spare, dark faces, wearing the habitual homesick look, presented a pitiful spectacle. I noticed one, however, who had evidently grown callous or superior to his hard lot, and was ladling soup from an open kettle in the pouring rain to his companions, with a grim disregard of surroundings or outraged stomachs.

We soon reached the dividing line between Idaho and Washington, and at eleven o'clock arrived at Spokane Falls. There the train made a halt of about half an hour, but from our point of view it was impossible to form any idea of the place further than that it had the natural promise of becoming a town of respectable dimensions, inasmuch as it was located, like many of our large cities, in a spot where nature never intended anything else to exist. I judged, too, that its citizens were equal to the task they had undertaken in attempting to build a town, as I noticed several places where the boulders, which cover the earth in many spots, had been carefully arranged in square groups and fenced in as a foundation upon which to build building lots. I afterwards made several visits to the city, of which mention is made farther on, and found my first judgment verified.

CHAPTER II.

Cheney, twenty miles west of Spokane Falls, was my point of disembarkation from the "overland" train, and is the junction with the Central Washington, which road I was to take for Wilbur, a small town in Lincoln county, in the "Big Bend country," and known to the earlier settlers and explorers as Wild Goose Bill's ranch. Arriving at Cheney about one o'clock, I sought the residence of Mrs. Lucy A. Switzer, president of the Eastern Washington W. C. T. U., but, finding her absent, presented my letters of introduction to her husband, who at once gave me a cordial welcome to Washington. Cheney is one of the older and also pleasanter towns of Washington east of the Cascade range of mountains, and is about two thousand feet above sea level. Evidences of volcanic eruptions are everywhere to be seen in the vicinity, the town itself being nearly surrounded by small lakes, which are but old craters filled with water. These lakes are to be found in all stages of advancement towards terra firma, from those having but a fringe of reeds at the edge, to those having but a small surface of water surrounded by a sedgy marsh. Many, too, have entirely grown in and formed solid earth upon which towns are now standing, having been built there from the attractions of level ground and water, which last is always to be found in those places. Timber is found wherever there is water, and the most pleasing natural feature of Cheney is its pine trees.

After a stop of about three hours, I took the train for Wilbur, arriving about ten o'clock the same night. Upon inquiring for a hotel, a sleepy-looking boy, sitting on the front seat of a mud-bespattered spring wagon, said, "This yer's the hack," and invited me to get in.

But that was a feat beyond my training in physical culture; as the "hack" stood three or four feet from the platform, and the platform was about the same distance from the ground. Seeing the situation, the station agent finally came to my assistance, and the dejected team of "cayuses" was induced to back up within reach. The hotel was a building of, perhaps, a dozen rooms, constructed entirely of rough fir lumber, and not furnished with all the modern conveniences; but when the proprietor told me he was born in Ohio, and was "awful glad to see anybody from there," and that he would give me the best room he had vacant, although it was "no great shucks," I felt such a sense of relief from concern regarding my unknown surroundings that the remaining discomforts seemed of small importance.

In the morning I was awakened by voices beside my window, and peeping out, saw that a party of Indians mounted on ponies had halted there to decide some question, the purport of which I could not catch. The squaws fluttered their bright blankets by rapid gesticulations, the males shook their heads in stubborn disapproval, and I concluded the grotesqueness of the scene was sufficient recompense for my broken slumber, although I had felt much impatience at being disturbed. After breakfast, having to wait for a conveyance to go into the country, I took a seat on the rude, unshaded platform at the front of the hotel, and passed the time till noon in making inquiries of the proprietor, his wife and others regarding the country, and answering questions concerning the East.

"I'd like to go East, but I wouldn't like to be struck by lightnin'," said a lithe-looking young man as he sat on the edge of the platform amusing himself by whirling a lariat, which persistently fell short of the mark, toward the faintly animate skeleton of a "cayuse" tethered near.

Thinking the expression "struck by lightning" contained some Western witticism with which I was not yet familiar, I asked for an explanation, and found that among the people born west of the Rocky Mountains, where thunderstorms seldom occur, one of the prevailing impressions regarding the East is that people are in imminent danger of losing their lives by lightning. Highly amused, I told the young man that as he had thus far escaped being "struck by a rattler" while threading the Columbia's rocky banks, but a few miles distant, Eastern lightning should have no terrors for him, but could not overcome the delusion. Another idea indulged in by natives of the Pacific Slope is that during the summer, Eastern people suffer greatly from lack of sleep, on account of the excessive heat. The full absurdity of this latter idea did not dawn upon my mind until in July, when, after retiring with the thermometer near a hundred, I would be awakened by a sense of cold that could only be overcome by all the blankets necessary in December. Having a preference for heat rather than cold, and remembering the luxurious temperature of properly ventilated rooms in the East in July, I was not, probably, a fair subject for conversion to the belief that the West was "the best country in the world to sleep in," as Western people asseverate.

Wilbur is, or, rather, was at the time of my

arrival, a halting place for miners going to and from the Salmon River mines; for bands of Indians in their ceaseless and, apparently, aimless ramblings; and the trading point for farmers and ranchmen for many miles around. Numerous saloons furnish sufficient water of discord—openly to the whites and stealthily to the Indians—to keep the sound of gun-shots from entirely dying out, and, although such scenes were said to be on the wane, I was told that on the last Fourth of July, the Indians, filled with liquor furnished by their civilized white brothers, had executed a style of war-dance through the streets that sent men, women and children to the shelter of the cabins, with heads "ducked" to dodge bullets and none of the grace of the holiday promenade in their gaits.

Soon after noon a young man arrived to take me into the country, and I prepared for a trip of nine miles by wagon. We were soon out on the rolling, bunch-grass plains, and as the day was bright, everything seemed auspicious except a breeze from the north, which was thought to be a balmy zephyr by my companion, but which in striking my face brought the sensation of being pierced by numbers of fine needle points. I afterwards learned that such was the experience of many newcomers, but nobody had discovered the cause. Noticing a general absence of water as we passed along, I asked how stock could live in such a country.

"Oh, there are some springs, but the cattle go to the draws as long as there is any water in them. and then they go to the river," was the answer.

"What is a draw?" I asked.

"Why, they are—a draw is—well, Corby's draw is just ahead, and you can see it for yourself," said my companion.

We soon came to a grassy pond similar to those produced by spring freshets everywhere, but called a "draw" in eastern Washington for some reason which nobody could explain. These ponds dry out as soon as the spring rains cease, and leave the surface of the country destitute of water except that coming from springs, which are truly "few and far between." Yet, water is found at a depth of from fifteen to fifty feet below the surface in most parts of the Big Bend country, and the great need seems to be drilling apparatus that will withstand the broken volcanic rock into which it is necessary to pierce.

Four miles from our destination we came to Hesseltine, a town consisting of a deserted cottage and a rough board cabin, or "shack," as those buildings are often called, in which a postoffice was kept by a woman. A small tent, just large enough for a single cot, was pitched near the postoffice, and a "buckskin" pony, which means, simply, a pony of a yellow color, was hitched to a post as we drove up and asked for the mail for the ranch to which I was going. As a large bundle of Sunday School literature was handed out, I began to wonder where a sufficient number of children could be found to receive instruction from it, but was assured there were "plenty of children," which I found to be true, not only in that vicinity, but everywhere in the West. Children swarm on the Pacific Slope almost as thick as the salmon in the streams, but there are few dullards among them. No matter how meagre the opportunities for acquiring knowledge chanced to be, native ability beamed out from youthful eyes everywhere; and the great charm of Western childhood is that it is a youthful, and not an adult childhood, such as is often seen in the East.

As we neared the ranch, the aspect of the country improved, the ground being covered with flowers of all hues, and the bunch grass seeming to have doubled in height and fullness.

I spoke of the change, and my companion remarked, "Yes, mother took up the claim herself and got a good one. It has a living spring on it besides;" which, considering the rare combination of living water and fertility, in that country of uncertain possibilities, I accepted as a compliment to woman's judgment.

After remaining at the ranch a few days, I concluded to purchase a saddle horse with which to view the country; as such a thing as a road-cart or light buggy was not to be found within fifty miles. So I sent for an Indian trader, and the next evening a man rode up leading a strong, chestnut pony profusely decorated with hieroglyphics left on his shining coat by the branding irons of different owners. Prompted by my friends, I began the list of questions said to be necessary for a purchase.

"Will he buck?" I asked.

"No, lady, I don't think he'll buck. He don't buck with me, and I had a young lady ride him yesterday," was the answer.

In view of the *sotto voce* remark of one of my friends that the young lady referred to would mount a pony that "never knew a cinch," the answer was not reassuring, but I persevered.

"Will he bite?"

"Well, really I don't just know, but you might be on the lookout."

"Is he sound?"

"Yes, I believe he is perfectly sound."

"What do you ask for him?"

"Fifteen dollars. He's worth twenty-five."

Feeling that horse buying under such circumstances was but a lottery, with fair chances for breaking one's neck, I concluded to end the farce of questioning, and offered the man ten dollars, which he readily accepted and rode away over the hills.

Having the pony turned into a field for the night, the next morning I learned the full import of the advice, "First catch your hare." No amount of cajoling would bring that pony's forelock within grasping distance, and finally he had to be captured by stretching a rope with a man at each end and forcing him into a corner, where he lacerated himself on the sharp wires of the fence before submitting to the bridle. Yet I rode him eight miles the same day, and found him so susceptible to kindness that, although the outbound journey was marked by some vicious plunges and stubborn refusals to answer the rein, the homeward trip was made in perfect harmony, with occasional backward glances by the pony, evidently made to convince himself as to what new sort of passenger he carried, who did not strike him with cruel spurs nor belabor him with knotted rope. These "cayuses," as they are called, are very wise little animals, and when properly treated are as kind as wise; the disposition to kick, bite or "buck" being but the natural instinct of self preservation. They are burdened with heavy saddles, girted, or "cinched," as it is called in the West, to a state of breathlessness and then mounted and lacerated with murderous rowels till a merciful person experiences a feeling of actual delight upon seeing a rider shot out over a "bucking" head and landed ignominiously in the dust.

At the end of a few weeks, having received letters from Mrs. Switzer, I very regretfully parted with my pony, and returning to Wilbur, took the train for Davenport, in the same county, which place I was to make my headquarters while organizing W. C. T. Unions and filling lecture appointments in the Big Bend country.

CHAPTER III.

Arriving at Davenport, I found it to be a somewhat older town than Wilbur, having once been the county seat, and being the point from which supplies were shipped by wagon for Fort Spokane, on the Columbia, twenty-five miles distant. Finding the treasurer of the E. Washington W. C. T. U., Mrs. Rena G. McArthur, whose husband, Rev. J. A. McArthur, was pastor of the Presbyterian church, I soon secured quarters and awaited the action of the State president. On her arrival, arrangements were made that Mrs. C. H. Pryor, county superintendent of schools for Lincoln county and also W. C. T. U. vice-president for the same, should take charge of the matter of appointments in her territory. Not having met Mrs. Pryor, I immediately pictured her in my mind as a woman nearing middle age, and as a consequence, when I was called to the parlor on her arrival, I was somewhat surprised to see a small figure with a bright, open, girlish face rise to meet me. But I soon discovered there was sufficient ability and determination in the makeup of the owner to carry her through the performance of any duty she would willingly assume. Mrs. Pryor is the county school superintendent whose third election to that office was contested the following autumn on the ground of ineligibility, and led to the decision of the Washington courts that women, although voters on school matters, could not legally hold office in the state.

"Egypt will be first on the list of appointments," said Mrs. Pryor, and seeing me smile as the suggestion the name brought came to me, added, "but it is not a place of darkness."

So, to Egypt I journeyed by stage a few mornings afterward. The town of Egypt, or, more properly, settlement, is on the stage road from Davenport to Fort Spokane and lies in one of the most pleasant and productive sections of Eastern Washington. The principal product is wheat, and the yield promised to be enormous. I had seen no native trees for several weeks, but now passed through lovely pine groves, and as I inhaled the grateful terebinthine odor, I thanked Mrs. Pryor in my heart for sending me to Egypt. She afterwards told me she had made that appointment first, with a view to counteracting any unpleasant impression I might have received of the country ; from which it may be inferred that the impressions received by strangers are not always highly pleasing.

I found my hostess at Egypt an intelligent young woman who had gone to the West as a teacher, and having married one of the many bachelor land owners, was the mistress of a pleasant home, made doubly inviting by order and artistic taste. There being no church building, the meeting was held in the schoolhouse, which was filled to overflowing. A man was chosen to introduce the speaker, but being rather deaf, and, consequently, not catching his hastily given instructions clearly, he performed his task by making the announcement, "Mrs. Scott, of Spokane Falls, will now address the meeting on the important subject of temperance."

I was somewhat surprised by that sudden transformation of my identity and place of residence, but managed to at once put in a disclaimer to any desire to appear under an alias. At the close of the meeting I succeeded in organizing a Union, nearly all of the principal women becoming members. On our way home we were suddenly halted by the balking of one of the half-broken horses of a span just ahead of ours, and a number of mothers having babes with them, my hostess among them, were on the ground in a moment. The night was intensely dark, and being entirely ignorant of my surroundings, I concluded to court no new dangers, but risk the stampeding of our own team, which seemed to be the fear, and remain in the wagon. That proved to be the better plan, as matters soon quieted down, but the babies had been so hopelessly mixed in the darkness that much time was consumed in restoring them to their respective mammas. Under such circumstances as those were the wide awake Washington women raising future presidents and at the same time casting their influence into the balance against unrighteousness, that the realm over which those same presidents shall hold the scepter may be one of order, love, and justice; instead of confusion, greed and oppression.

I next visited Harrington and Larene, both reached by stage, and then, returning to Wilbur, held meetings and organized there and proceeded on down the Central Washington R. R. to Almira, from which place I went twenty-three miles by stage to Coulee City. By this time the weather had become very hot, the mercury often running above a hundred in the shade at midday, and as the alkali dust was so dense as to be stifling, it will readily be understood that the trip to the latter place was not an inspiring one.

Yet, as we were passing through a narrow defile between the rocks to get into the town, a man, flushed and dusty, stepped from behind a big, black boulder and asked if I was the lady who was going to lecture. I told him such was my intention, upon which he said: "All right!

We've always been disappointed before by lecturers not coming as they agreed, so we have not done anything but give out the notice. But the boys will work lively when they know you are here."

He then told the driver to take me to a certain hotel, and, as we passed on, I wondered who "the boys" could possibly be, and why they should work more lively for my coming. But I had not long to wait for the answer. Before I had fully shaken off the dust of the ride, the same man appeared at the hotel bringing another with him, whom he introduced as the editor of the "Coulee City News." Then the fact came out that there had never yet been a public meeting in the town except a Sunday School, which had been held in the dining-room of the hotel I was then in.

"But," said the editor, who had, evidently, been made chairman of the "committee on arrangements," "now you are here, and we know there will be no disappointment, we'll get the boys together this afternoon, and clean out a new store building that has just been put up, and by night we'll have it in trim for a meeting." He then told me that but two nights previous a shooting affray in which the inmates of a saloon and house of ill fame had participated had occurred in the street, to the terror of respectable citizens, and consequently they were glad to welcome those whose efforts were directed against such outrages.

Mrs. E. A. Foreman, wife of the proprietor of the hotel, in speaking of the difficulties in the way of keeping a respectable, temperance house, remarked incidentally, "Mr. Foreman and I have often retired fearing our house would be burned over us before morning," which will give some idea of the state of lawlessness existing.

The editor was successful in getting his "boys" together, and when night came I was escorted to a new building, in which rough boards had been placed for seats and a crowd of dusty men and women was fast gathering. To my surprise, two women, with garments heavily laden with dust, stepped up and displayed the white ribbon, telling me they had driven many miles for the sake of attending the meeting. After the usual opening exercises, the editor made a little introductory speech, in which he paid a high compliment to the W. C. T. U., and told the audience to bear in mind and carry into the history of the town the fact that a woman had braved the hardships of the trip and made the first public speech in Coulee City. The place was oppressively warm, and as I looked over the heads of the audience into the lingering twilight outside, great clouds of the flour-like dust met my gaze as they swept past; but, as I thought of the enthusiasm and frankly expressed kindness of those who had such discomforts to endure continually, my own small ills fell into insignificance, and were lost sight of in the effort to prove helpful to the brave hearts who were making such a stand against evil while battling with physical ills quite inconceivable to those who have never experienced them.

Returning to Davenport, where an appointment awaited me, I found that another had been made at a school house some eight miles distant, to which Mrs. Pryor was to convey me by carriage. One of the greatest sources of irritation an Eastern person, in the habit of counting minutes, meets with in some parts of the West is the general inclination to be late everywhere and under all circumstances ; and having had some experience in that direction, I began to grow uneasy as the afternoon before the evening of the latter appointment wore on toward twilight without Mrs. Pryor making her appearance. Finally she arrived, but the first mile on the road gave so little promise of our reaching our destination at the proper time that I drew my watch in apprehension.

Seeing the action, Mrs. Pryor asked in some surprise, "What time is it?"

Being told, she remarked that she had not

driven more rapidly for fear the roughness of the road would weary me.

"Never mind me; drive on!" I answered, in desperation, as thoughts of a deserted school house and disgusted country people flashed through my mind.

Then Mrs. Pryor verified the estimate I had formed of her character, and I was treated to a display of Western horsewomanship such as is seldom witnessed. Realizing that the time was short, she coolly remarked, "We'll get there," and with eyes and hands alert to guide the carriage clear of rocks, proceeded to let out her span of bays at a rate that soon rivaled the speed indulged in by the most reckless of Jehus whose driving I had tested, and brought forcibly to mind the story of Horace Greeley's ride to Placerville in the hands of Hank Monk. I made no note of the time in which we covered the distance, but it is needless to say that we "got there."

At the close of the meeting, we were invited to spend the night at a stock ranch near, owned and conducted by women. On arriving and being introduced to the ladies—a Mrs. Green and her three daughters—I at once began making inquiries as to the manner of conducting, and the success attending such an enterprise when entirely in the hands of the weaker sex. In answer, one of the young ladies displayed a neatly kept set of stock books, showing the age, lineage and name of every animal on the ranch, and told me that the keeping of the books was her especial duty.

"How did you succeed in bringing your stock through the winter?" I asked, remembering the many carcasses of cattle I had seen strewn over the country, and having been told that many thousands had perished.

"We have never lost a head from hunger or cold," she answered, and then added, with decision: "There is no need of stock starving or freezing in this country. The cause of such things is always bad management."

"Upon further conversation, I learned that but one man was employed on the ranch except during the seeding and harvesting seasons, and that the women, who were refined and educated, managed every detail of the business.

CHAPTER IV.

On returning to Davenport, I found letters calling me to Spokane and Whitman counties, which necessitated a change of headquarters. So I said good-bye to the Big Bend country and started for Cheney, stopping at several points on the way, but leaving Medical Lake, a place of some importance, for a future date. Establishing my headquarters at Cheney, I first visited Spokane Falls in company with the State president, and there met Mrs. Esther A. Jobes, superintendent of the Department of Literature of the East Washington W. C. T. U., and one of the brightest women I met in the West. Mrs. Olive H. Bowen, superintendent of the Department of Work Among Miners, drove us over to Ross Park, the pride of Spokane Falls, and its one aristocratic suburb. I did not discover the "park," but when I thought of the amount of labor necessary to produce even the small number of beautiful green lawns to be seen, from a natural surface so rocky and brown as that surrounding them, I felt that the Spokanites were justified in their estimate of the merits of the spot. A large building for an interstate exposition which was to be held the following October was being erected at the Falls, and after securing space in it for a representation of the W. C. T. U., we returned to Cheney.

I visited Spokane several times afterwards and had opportunities of judging of its progress and prosperity. To judge of the former, after learning the age of the city, all that was necessary was to watch the crowding throngs in its streets and glance at its beautiful buildings. Nearly all of the business structures are of brick or stone, and beautiful decorations of different varieties of chalcedony and other handsome stones shine out on the fronts of some and on many private dwellings. As to the latter, the ultimate prosperity of the place is assured by its surroundings. The great mineral wealth of the hills combined with the remarkable productiveness of the arable land cannot fail to prove a source of revenue sufficient to support a large city. The location of the town itself suggests the idea that none but giants, physical and mental, could ever have wrought a town out of such material. But Spokane has its giants, of both kinds, and it possesses an amount of stubborn will not easily overcome, as was shown while I was in the vicinity. When the Exposition Building was nearing completion and the time for opening was drawing near, the workmen, through some fault of the contract, concluded to indulge in a strike. But the "great show" was not to be delayed by any such disloyal conduct. The professional and business men of the town marched to the grounds in squads and, with an utter disregard of the fate of silk hats and fine clothes, took up hatchet and saw and proceeded with the work.

Starting from Spokane Falls on the Union Pacific R. R., my first stopping point was Rockford, after which followed Fairfield, Latah, Tekoa, Farmington, Garfield, Colfax, Oakesdale, Rosalia, Pine City, St. Johns, Palouse City, Pullman and Colton. The largest of these towns is Colfax, at which place I stopped four days. Colfax is in Whitman county, which is called the banner wheat county of Washington. The town is inclosed by almost perpendicular walls of rock, which literally stand in the way of expansion, and unless some style of architecture of the barnacle order shall be invented, the future seems to promise Colfax nothing in the way of growth. One of the chief branches of trade carried on is that of furnishing harvesting machinery, but there are good dry-goods, drug and other stores, and the people are not lacking in enterprise and intelligence. I there met Mrs. Dr. Boswell, Mrs. L. M. Carley and others well known in moral public circles, and at Palouse City I had the pleasure of meeting Mrs. Judge Buck, formerly Territorial president of Idaho, and Mrs. Mary E. Beach, who divides her time between that place and Colfax in looking after the management of her estates in both places. At Pullman, I met Rev. Elvira Cobleigh, who was at the time pastor of the Congregational church, and whose debtor I was made by her thoughtful assistance. Owing to some misunderstanding, no one met me at the station at Pullman, and, there being no carriages, I was obliged to walk a long distance through the dust and climb a sky-reaching bluff at the last. As a consequence I was both physically and mentally irritated when Mrs. Cobleigh reached me ; but my disquiet was soon assuaged by her helpful words and presence.

Aside from the large wheat fields, which stretch up the hillsides to a height that would prove disastrous where rain-falls are frequent, there is little of interest in the "Palouse country," as the great wheat section is called. Some of the towns are given attractive, but truth compels me to say, misleading, names. For instance, Oakesdale has no oaks—in fact, no native trees of any kind; Rosalia is barren of roses, and, while there are pines at Pine City, there does not happen to be any city. I reached the latter place by stage, which was an open buggy drawn by two ponies, one of which persisted in leading the other by half a length, and both of which persisted in running down hill at a perilous rate. They seemed to be quite beyond the control of the driver, who was much past seventy years of age, but he explained, by way of apology for the apparent recklessness, that it was only in going down hill that any speed could be made. I knew such to be the fact, inasmuch as the moment we finished the descent of one hill we began the ascent of another; and so I followed the example of my aged companion, who sat erect and gazed upward, evidently not wishing to contemplate the danger of being thrown from the dizzy heights by the breaking of a belt or buckle. The fortitude necessary to endure the short mail-route trips is as nothing, however, to that called for on the regular passenger and freight stage lines. On some of the regular lines on which I traveled, the vehicles, which were strong, three-seated open wagons, were first examined to make sure that nothing should break under any probable strain; bags, boxes and packages were then placed under the seats; numerous mail pouches were stacked in the rear and securely lashed on, and then the passengers crowded themselves into the remaining space. The progress up hill was necessarily slow, but, upon reaching the top, the brakes would be put on, and the team, usually of four horses, would be lashed into a gait that rendered clinging to the seat rail a necessity, and often left one's body ornamented with contusions; the latter being the result of being thrown against the sides of the box or seat by the wheels striking rocks or dropping into "chuck holes;" which last are holes abruptly indented in soft spots of the dry earth by the wheels of the still heavier freight wagons.

About the middle of September, I returned to Cheney, soon afterwards visiting Medical Lake, which was fast becoming popular as a summer resort. I there enjoyed the hospitality of Mrs. Jennie L. Green, through whose courtesy I was rowed across the lake, where I visited the Eastern Washington Asylum for the Insane, which stands in a grove of pines on an eminence sloping down to the water's edge. The lake is similar to those about Cheney, except that it has the appearance of being of more recent creation, no sign of vegetable growth being as yet visible inside its rocky rim. The water is so thoroughly impregnated with potash that no fish can live in it, but Nature, from the unlimited resources of an illimitable wisdom, has peopled it with myriads of small, red insects, which, dying, drop upon the bare rock ledges of its sloping sides in a sort of pulp, thus forming a base for vegetable growth. In earlier times both Indians and whites utilized the water in the practical art of soap-making, but it was found to possess great curative power over some diseases, and is now used for medicinal purposes alone.

Returning still again to Cheney, I made preparation for my trip over the Cascade Mountains to what is called Western Washington, my first objective point after crossing the Cascades being Port Townsend, on Puget Sound. My first stopping place after leaving Cheney was Sprague, the county seat of Lincoln county, and, like Cheney, one of the older towns in Eastern Washington. Being a division station of the Northern Pacific R. R., it is what may be called a railroad town, and its inhabitants are largely railroad employes. I there found traces of the efforts of Mrs. Mary Clement Leavitt, the far-seeing, patient and able W. C. T. U. path-beater, who was, at the time of my visit to Sprague, bearing her torch through highways and byways far beyond the Pacific, on her way around the world. The Union at Sprague was only a memory, but, resurrecting it and placing two pastors' wives "at the fore", I proceeded to Ritzville, in Adams county. Ritzville is at the eastern edge of the sage brush plains of Eastern Washington, and its principal natural features are black boulders, bunch grass and sage intermingled, and a sandy but productive soil. Wondering why a town should be built in such a spot, and knowing that minerals were found at some depth in many places in the section, I asked if gold or silver had been discovered near.

"No," said my hostess, Mrs. A. C. Singer, wife of the Congregational pastor, "we have not found either yet, but one of our townsmen has just discovered what he hopes will prove a gold mine, in the form of a vein of polishing powder."

She then showed me some of the powder, which had been discovered at a depth of a few feet on digging a well, and which appeared to me to be sand ground to a state of impalpability, probably by some mill of nature long gone out of use. But its merits as a polishing powder were apparent on applying it to gold, silver or tin surfaces, and arrangements were being made for placing it on the market.

North Yakima, a hundred and seventy miles farther on the way, came next on the list, and after traveling over dry sage brush plains until I was weary of the view, I was agreeably surprised on arriving to find myself in a beautiful little town, full of trees and other vegetation (produced by irrigation), and with streets thronged with intelligent and progressive people. While there I learned that efforts had been and were still being made to bring the state capital to that place; and, considering its geographical location, which is near the center of the state, and also the fact that it is easy of access by rail, it has much in its favor above Olympia, the present capital.

My next stop was to have been at Ellensburg, but when on my way to that place, our train drew up in a wild, rocky glen at about four o'clock in the afternoon, and the passengers were told to prepare for a delay of five hours. Learning that a freight train was derailed a short distance ahead of ours, and that there was small hope of the track being cleared even in the time specified, I concluded to go through to Tacoma, where I was to take the steamer for Port Townsend. As the change of plan necessitated a re-checking of my baggage, I looked about for some one of the trainmen of whom to ask the favor of taking my checks to the baggage car, but found all had availed themselves of the opportunity for relief from the routine of daily duties, and were exploring the surroundings with the passengers. Indeed, the delay seemed to be so highly enjoyed by the weary "overlanders" that it was a pleasure to watch their movements as they promenaded in squads or climbed among the rocks in search of "specimens". Finally, after trudging the distance to the baggage cars of the long train in sand several inches deep, I succeeded in re-checking my baggage, and then, as darkness was coming on, sought rest for the night.

CHAPTER V.

While in Eastern Washington, I had heard so many conflicting opinions expressed of the country west of the Cascades that my mind was in a state of confused imbecility regarding it.

"If you like a country where it rains all the time, you'll like it west of the mountains," said some.

"It is just as dry over there as it is here," others would say.

"Why, I wouldn't live over there, where you have to wade in mud and grub ferns all the time, if they'd give me the country," said a ranchman whom I met at Cheney.

But while I was trying to decide in my mind whether the pleasure of seeing fresh ferns would or would not counterbalance the mud, a commercial traveler present, taking advantage of the ranchman's inattention for a moment, remarked, impressively, "When you get west of the Cascades you'll be in a white country."

I make these quotations as some excuse to the reader for my feeble state of mind as I fell asleep while the train was lying under a low bluff of dry, red rock in the glen west of North Yakima, and not as an insinuation that Western people lack veracity. Tastes differ, and the vision is often biased by other senses; and with something of that thought in my mind, I caught my first glimpse of Washington west of the Cascade Mountains. But I was not prepared for the sensation that first sight produced. No one who has not for five consecutive months of the warmer season traveled over a country never fully supplied with water, can possibly understand the gratitude, relief and sense of rising energy I felt as I looked out at break of day and saw that we were passing through dense undergrowth interspersed with monster yews, and ferns higher than one's head, all dripping with pearly moisture. I at once decided in favor of the ferns as against the mud, but after observation convinced me that ferns of such dimensions were much more restful to the eyes of sightseers than to the spinal column of those engaged in their extermination. Yet, as the balmy air from the moist foliage began to relax the tense nervous strain incident to the atmosphere and altitude out of which I had come, a firm and lasting conviction settled upon my mind that, though the ferns shot up in a night, as the people claim they do, and grew as high as the yews above them, I would still prefer that state of affairs to the other extreme—on the principle that a continual surfeit is safer than a protracted fast.

We arrived at Tacoma at about eight o'clock in the morning, being just in time for the Port Townsend boat. As we drew out of the harbor into the open water, I began to realize the extent of that wonderful inland salt water sea, Puget Sound. The day was showery and a light breeze was blowing from the north, but when I went on deck I found that both showers and breeze would in Ohio belong more properly to the after part of April than the middle of October. The steamer was crowded with passengers, several of whom were on the last stretch of the long overland trip from points east of Chicago, and who, unmindful of the rain that beat against them, stood and gazed in speechless wonder at the scene that had opened before them. After the first glimpse, I returned to the cabin and, drawing on a heavy coat, armed myself with an umbrella and again sought the deck, determined to lose nothing of the wonderful panorama, made up of blue water beneath; flocks of beautiful gulls sweeping down almost within reach, from above ; islands and mainland embossed with the verdure of the *madrono* tree and fringed and tasseled with the delicate foliage of the cedar and fir ; and shifting mist effects of which the eye would never tire.

"What do you think of it, Jennie?" asked a young husband of the cultured but delicate wife he had brought from her Pennsylvania home to share another with him on the shore of Bellingham Bay.

"Is it all like this?" was the cautious prelude to Jennie's answer.

"Oh, yes," the husband replied, but, with the true Western spirit of rivalry, added, "only, I think it is better where our place is."

Turning her eyes from the scene before her to her husband, the young wife answered, with deliberation, "Then I think I shall remain."

Discovering that the little side scene had not escaped my observation, the couple explained, between them, that the husband had left college three years before to seek a place where he could make a home for his then affianced and himself; had wrestled with Fortune two years alone, but in the third had so far gained the mastery that he had gone back for his promised wife, who then stood beside him, but whose parents had parted with their daughter with some misgivings regarding the safety and comfort of a country full of Indians and unplastered houses.

As we neared Port Townsend, the clouds broke away and let in the sunlight, and the most beautiful rainbow I remember having seen reared its variegated arch to view over our starboard quarter as we steamed into the harbor, past vessels from Japan and other points on the shores of the wide Pacific.

Having while in Eastern Washington held some correspondence with Mrs. Emma Barrett, who is, probably, the most successful evangelist, male or female, west of the Rocky Mountains, and who established the Seaman's Home at Port Townsend, I inquired for her on my arrival, and was directed to her residence. Having known her in former years, when as Emma Molloy she held vast audiences spell-bound as she spoke in the cause of temperance ; and having from a distance offered my single mite of comfort when, later, she was reviled and hounded by servile agents of the liquor traffic and forsaken by time-serving comrades, I was pleased upon hearing, even before reaching her abode, that she was to preach in the Methodist Church both morning and evening of the following day, which was Sunday. Later I was introduced to her husband, Mr. Morris Barrett, for many years in the Government printing office at Washington, D. C., and still owning a home there, although now on the Port Townsend *Leader*, and found him in full sympathy with his wife's works and views. Their house is always open to those in want, whether physical or mental. and as I again and again returned to Port Townsend and noted the variety of wants filled and the number of hearts comforted, it occurred to me that a not inappropriate inscription to be placed over the doorway of that home would be the lines from Elizabeth Whittier's beautiful poem Charity,

> "Whoever thou art whose need is great,
> In the name of Christ, the compassionate,
> And merciful one, for thee I wait."

After remaining a week in Port Townsend, I started out to fill appointments in the towns of the Sound, my first point being New Dungenness, on the Straits of San Juan de Fuca. To reach that place I was obliged to take a steamer for Port William, simply a wharf built out from the rocky shore, where I was to be met with a private conveyance and taken five miles across the country. Although New Dungenness had been entered by the lighter draft local steamers since the advent of steam on the Sound, rivalry of interests had resulted in such a deception, or bias, or whatever it may have been, of the postal officials at the national capital, that they had created a post-office at Port William, a postal route from there to New Dungenness, and had given instructions that no mail be delivered by boat at the latter place. By such arrangement property near Port William was enhanced in value, but the Dungennessites were compelled to haul their produce five miles for shipment and endure many other inconveniences caused by the change.

Mr. Charles Davis, the proprietor of a large dairy farm near New Dungenness harbor, and at whose house I was to stop, accompanied me from Port Townsend, and a brother, Mr. William Davis, who owns another dairy farm three miles from the first, met us at Port William. As we drove along through the deep forest of monster firs and cedars, the brothers, seeing my interest in the surroundings, told me of the still earlier days, when they had come, with their wives, into the then unbroken wilderness, and, clearing away the gigantic trees, had raised produce, which they marketed, at Post Townsend and others of the older ports, in small yachts sailed by themselves.

Many of the trees between which we were passing were over two hundred feet high, and a number to which my attention was called were said to measure from seven to ten feet in diameter. Yet, some of the enormous cedars reached down their delicate. fern-like leaves within grasp, and I severed a number of perfect specimens as we passed under the boughs.

At a gateway about a quarter of a mile from Mr. Davis' residence, we found Mrs. Davis awaiting to welcome me to their "home by the sea," which I found to be a modern square-roofed mansion, set in grounds embellished with shrubs bearing masses of scarlet berries and as perfect in its interior appointments as sterling English housekeeping and a model Chinese cook could make it. To the left as one faces the water, which is within plain sight of the house, lie the long salt marshes, upon which the cows graze the entire year, and without which dairy farming would be an Herculean task in that section of country. The Olympic Mountains, with their crests of snow, are also within plain view of Mr. Davis' residence, and while gazing at them I utilized the time by picking handfuls of delicious blackberries from the native "evergreen" bushes at the back of the house. And this was in the latter part of October.

The next morning after my arrival, as we were on our way to church, great numbers of large black birds circled around and over the carriage, and I asked, quite innocently, "What kind of birds are those?"

Everybody laughed, and Mr. Davis, answering that they were crows, asked, in great astonishment, "Don't you know a crow?"

"Not of that size," I answered, and added that crows did not grow to the size of turkeys in the East.

Then the laugh was in my favor, and I ventured to ask if crows of such dimensions were not very destructive to crops. In reply I was told that they fed on the small crustaceous animals and shellfish brought in or left bare by the tides, and, moreover, that they were looked upon with great reverence by the Indians, who believed that when one of their race died, his spirit at once took up its habitation in a crow.

After spending one night with the family of Mr. William Davis, and becoming acquainted with his most estimable wife, I returned to Port William preparatory to taking the steamer to Port Angeles, still farther out towards the ocean. As I sat on the lone wharf waiting for the coming of the boat, a fleet of Indian canoes, the sight of which, with their untamed occupants, would have driven an artist wild with delight, drew in towards the shore and finally stopped but a few feet from me. They were loaded with fish and clams, and both Indians and squaws seemed highly pleased over their remarkable catch. Soon they passed around the wharf, and steering up to the bank under a shelving bluff, fastened their boats and prepared to camp for the night, it then being past four o'clock.

Finally the steamer arrived, and securing a camp stool, I seated myself on the forward deck, that I might catch all the remaining daylight. Fixing my eyes on the sunset, which was a sight to be remembered as a dream of what may be in the hereafter, I had almost lost thought of my immediate surroundings, when I became conscious that others were gathering around me and all eyes were turned in the same direction as my own. Looking at my companions, I saw such a mixed company as is seldom seen outside of the large cities. Close at my side stood a young girl, who, having attended one of my Port Townsend meetings, had recognized me as I came on board, and who gladly imparted to me what knowledge she had of our fellow passengers.

"You see those two men there, in gray clothes, by the rail?" she said, interrogatively.

I nodded an affirmative, and she continued: "They belong to the infidel colony up at Angeles."

Having previously heard that a community which held up as one of its tenets the paradox, "No saloons nor churches," existed somewhere in the vicinity, I at once understood the pertinence of the information, and again looked at the two men, who seemed, somehow, to have missed life's sunshine, but whose eyes were intently bent on the sinking orb before us. With the thought, which was a prayer as well, that the sight then gazed upon might be but the imperfect type of one that would greet their vision when, in life's later days, with eyes cleared of earth's shadows, they would look out into former void and be met by the resplendent light of God's spirit, I turned towards two nuns sitting near and looked an interrogation at my companion.

"They are going to Angeles to see about the Catholic hospital there," was the answer to my mute question, and my young friend continued: "That man with the silk hat is trying to get an office—I forget what—and he's around 'lectioneering. That big man with the heavy chain has got a brewery at Seattle, or somewhere, and those two men ahead of him are from Mexico, I heard them say."

Two young men from Scotland, an Irishman, a Russian and a Japanese, were also a part of our group, to which several of the boatmen were at last attracted, as we sat and gazed in deepening silence on the red waves of light, all admitting by our rapt admiration the existence of an all-powerful and all-loving Being, whose spirit had just touched us through our eyes.

We reached Port Angeles soon after sundown, and as my stopping place was near the young lady's home, we started out together, her father, who met her at the wharf, accompanying us. The darkness seemed to deepen as we proceeded, and I could not account for it until my companion stopped and remarked that we had reached "the stairs"; when I found that a bluff nearly a hundred feet high and almost perpendicular barred our way. The bluff was to be scaled by means of a stairway, the first flight of which contained about one hundred steps and was entirely devoid of hand rails. Moreover, the steps were slippery from recent rain, and a fall meant maiming and perhaps death on the rocks below. Yet, one soon learns the insufficiency of self-reliance under such circumstances, and I made the first step with much the same feeling of resignation that I had once grasped the lower rungs of a rope ladder, thrown over a ship's side, with a restless yawl under my feet and pitch-like darkness, aggravated by a driving snow-storm, about me. We reached the first landing, caught our breath and toiled on until we finally gained the summit, where we stood and strained our eyes to get a glimpse of the electric lights at Victoria, B. C., just across the Straits. The night-fog was too dense to be penetrated, but I was assured that in clearer weather the lights at Victoria were plainly visible from Port Angeles Heights.

After spending two very pleasant days at Port Angeles, I returned to Port Townsend, and while on my way I met and conversed with one of the "infidel colony" leaders, the substance of which conversation I give, to illustrate the fertility of the section as a field for evangelistic effort. Embarking at five o'clock in the morning, before the chilling fog had been dispersed, all the passengers were obliged to seek the small cabin, and while there a discussion as to the merits of Christianity arose between two men, one of whom gave expression to his doubts in such an outspoken manner as to arrest the attention of everybody. Placing him at once by his remarks, I determined to seek some information of the peculiar enterprise he was engaged in, and so, as soon as the fog lifted, and we went upon deck, I beckoned him to a stool beside me, and asked of the success of the colony. Without hesitation he frankly admitted that it was a signal failure.

"To what do you attribute your failure?" I asked.

"Well, to tell the truth," he answered, "the very selfishness, and greed—and pride, even, that we went there to escape, cropped out among ourselves."

Seeing the smile I could not repress, he said, dejectedly, "I suppose it does look funny to others, but it has been no joke to some of us."

I at once assured him that I had no intention to laugh at his misfortunes, but could not help smiling at his simplicity in thinking to escape the trio he had mentioned, upon which he broke out with, "What kind of a God is it that allows such things?"

Seeing that he was becoming excited, and wishing to give him time for the outburst of impatience to pass, I looked at the familiar gulls, which were flying so low as to almost touch our heads, and remarked that I would like to have one.

Thinking I wanted a bird killed, for the taxidermist, he said by way of answer, "You would never want but one. My wife thought she'd like one, and I shot one for her; but I didn't get over it for a week. It had the most pitiful look in its eyes you ever saw."

And that was the man who had just blasphemed his Maker, and was one of the leaders of the "infidel colony"! That glimpse of his true nature led to further inquiry, and I learned that he had been robbed of his birthright to parental care, by a drunken father and an overworked mother, at the outset, and later had floated out into the unfeeling world and far more cruel sea of doubt past the numerous church-doors of a great city, and no hand that he dared grasp had been reached out, and no voice he could understand had called to him as he drifted by.

Telling him wherein I thought the source of his whole trouble lay, I spoke of some simple methods by which he might bring his will into harmony with that of the Supreme Power, and was agreeably surprised by his quick look of comprehension and the remark, "Something like that has come to me once or twice when I've been thinking this matter over, and I've talked with my wife about it."

Finding him so near the light, but a few words more were necessary to get from him the promise that he would go home and tell his wife what had been said, and together they would give the new way a trial, at least.

CHAPTER VI.

Lopez Island, one of the San Juan group, was the next point to be visited, and I took the noon steamer from Port Townsend to Richardson, a new landing near the farm of Mr. James Davis, a brother to the dairy farmers of New Dungennes. I found Mr. Davis waiting to conduct me to the house, and as we walked along through a field where the clover formed a thick green mat, I remarked on the productiveness of the soil, and was told that it was impossible to over crop it. And I found such to be the case on all the islands wherever the surface was sufficiently concave to have retained the deposits of vegetable and animal matter left by the subsidence of the water, which once, without doubt, covered the entire country.

Mrs. Davis, whom I found to be an intelligent, well informed woman, and who was one of the W. Washington W. C. T. U. vice-presidents, gave me some interesting reminiscences, among which was the fact that she was the first white woman to live on the island. The annual meeting of the Lopez W. C. T. U. was held the next day after my arrival, which was on Friday, and from it I was to return with Mrs. Johnson, wife of Hon. G. M. Johnson, to her home at Lopez Harbor, on the opposite side of the island. As an election of school officers was to occur on the same day, the W. C. T. U. meeting was appointed for four o'clock in the afternoon, for the purpose of giving the members an opportunity to vote at the school election ; the Washington women having, as before incidentally mentioned, been granted that small privilege by the State constitution, after having enjoyed full suffrage in Washington as a territory for years. As four o'clock drew near, a number of women assembled, but Mrs. Johnson was not among them.

"Oh, you need not look for Mrs. Johnson yet," said one of the ladies. "Her ponies have been on the go all day taking voters to the polls, and she will be late."

It then come out that the temperance people were strongly opposed to one of the candidates, and Mrs. Johnson was rallying forces for his defeat. For the first time realizing that I was in a country where the women were "free born" and were still recognized as being "half white," I felt that I could wait for Mrs. Johnson's coming till the small hours of the morning, if necessary. I did not have so long to wait, but the night's experience proved sufficiently eventful as it transpired.

Just as the sun was dropping behind the tall firs, a span of white ponies were drawn up at the gate by a slender, alert-looking woman, whom I recognized intuitively as Mrs. Johnson, and who simply said, "We've won."

Such an announcement was sufficient recompense for all the delay, and hastening through the business of the meeting, good-nights were said, and Mrs. Johnson and I set out for Lopez Harbor. Taking into consideration that the trip was one of several miles; that the track ran through deep fir woods and wound in and out between tree boles so near that the wheels sometimes struck them in passing; that several pools of water had to be forded; that we were always going down hill when we were not going up; and that the darkness was so dense at several points that we could not see the white ponies before us, the fact that we reached our destination in safety may be looked upon as a feat in which human agency performed but a diminutive part.

We said little, as words seemed out of place; but at one point my companion's "nerve" seemed to fail her for a moment, and she turned to me with, "We're going into a gorge, but whether we are in the road or not, I do not know."

Recalling my training in horsemanship, I

suggested that she "give the ponies their heads," as they could see better than we.

She "amended the motion" by saying that she would also put on the brakes at such times as we should "feel" we were going down hill, and added that we would then have done all we could do.

Down we went into a deep gorge partly filled with water, through which the ponies waded and scrambled up the farther bank without let or hindrance from their driver. Soon afterwards Mrs. Johnson's quick ear caught the sound of a coming team, and as the track was single, with but few passing places for vehicles, our only chance of safety lay in an immediate halt. Drawing the ponies up, my companion called out into the darkness and found that the approaching wagon contained two men, which proved to be a fortunate circumstance. Investigation showed that we were in a place where passing was well-nigh impossible, but the two men together succeeded in lifting their wagon from the deep worn track to the rocks at its side, and good naturedly calling to us, "You'll make it, all right!" as encouragement for the rest of our journey, allowed us to pass on in safety.

The temperance people of Lopez had succeeded in entirely banishing intoxicating liquors from the island, which at the time of my visit was a sort of haven of refuge to those who were endeavoring to overcome the drink habit. But efforts were constantly being made to introduce the traffic, and constant vigilance was necessary to defeat them. Two daylight appointments several miles apart had been made for Sunday, that all the islanders might have an opportunity to attend the meetings, and the result was a full attendance at both. At those meetings, I for the first time noticed Indians in the audience; there being quite a sprinkling of dark faces among the white ones. And as I spoke with several of the Indian women and found them interested and earnest in moral work, I gave Lopez Island the credit of having furnished the first sample I had seen of what the Indians might become under Caucassian influence with "fire water" and its train of evils left out.

From Lopez I went to Friday Harbor, on San Juan Island, where the M. E. pastor who had conducted the Lopez meetings, and who was stationed at the former place, had kindly made an appointment. On arriving I was conducted to the residence of Mrs. Driggs, whose husband was formerly one of the King county officials but had sought the island from failing health, and had introduced the enterprise of prune raising. While passing the time until evening I made some inquiries and learned something of the fruit yield, for which the San Juan Islands are becoming noted. In speaking of the strawberry crop, my hostess incidentally remarked that from a certain spot, which looked to be no larger than an ordinary kitchen garden, they had shipped a large number of tons of berries, the exact figures of which I forbear giving in consideration of the credulity necessary to accept them as correct.

"Tons!" I exclaimed, and added, "You meant to say bushels, I suppose."

Laughing heartily, she answered, "No, tons! I had forgotten you were from the East, or I would have been looking for you to doubt our crop yield here."

She then told me that in preparing fresh berries for the table, she had often found it necessary to slice the larger ones, that they might absorb the sugar sufficiently to be palatable. Receiving the direct force of the tides, each of which bears its offering of warmth from the Japan Currents, the San Juan group of islands seem particularly adapted to fruit growing; the only detraction being that the unusual productiveness of the soil, combined with the atmospheric influences, perhaps, seems to conduce more to fecundity and expansion than to delicacy of flavor.

Starting in the early morning for East Sound, on Orcas Island, I found the scenery lovely enough to have tempted the most restless of nomads to pitch his tent for a permanent residence. The captain of the diminutive steamer kindly gave me a seat in the wheel-house, from whence I could catch the full effect of every jutting headland and beautiful strip of shore, and as we drew sharply around promontories and left one charming scene only to be met by another—scenes of mirror-like water surface with a breath of morning mist upon it, shut in by sloping banks covered with dark green firs interspersed with patches of various grasses and deciduous shrubs in all varieties of autumn coloring, I found myself wishing the short miles were leagues, and that no cares lay at the end, to break in on the memory of the morning's enchantment.

While at East Sound, where I remained two days, I had the much-coveted opportunity of enjoying a close view of the lovely *madrono* tree. This tree, which is also called the arbutus and belongs to the laurel family, has foliage similar in shade to that of the sassafras, and in addition to its beauty in that diretion, clusters of bright red berries hang upon its branches till mid-winter and the bark of the younger trees is of a deep flesh color. With its cheering, spring-like freshness, it is the most attractive tree of the northwestern forest; and its branches and berries are often used for decorative purposes.

But its beauty of scenery and the feats of production of its soil do not comprise all the attractions and advantages of the Puget Sound country. Acres and acres of oyster beds, producing a small bivalve something like the cove oyster, lie ready for the dredge; clams of many varieties—and sizes—may be had for the digging; large flocks of ducks start up from sheltered coves as the steamers pass; the water is full of fish, in size from the sturgeon down to the smelt; the forests are alive with game; and, last but not least to those who love pets and admire beauty and innocence combined, the rocks are often covered with seals, which will whimper and cringe in a most helpless manner when danger threatens, and can be so far domesticated as to follow a small boat around with the readiness of a family spaniel. In fact, the question, "How shall I live?" has been so fully answered by Nature that many of the inhabitants give so little thought to business as to be a source of wonderment to new comers.

An instance of the heedless inertness sometimes seen occurred as I was on my return to Port Townsend from East Sound, and took on such a ludicrous aspect as to remain vividly in my mind. There being no female passenger beside myself except a middle-aged squaw, who was being sent to visit her people by her white husband, and from whom I could get no audible expression except a guttural "Put Tonsen," and nothing but a stiff nod of comprehension as I pointed towards some object of interest, I was naturally anxious to reach my destination as soon as possible. The steamer was due at Port Townsend at eight o'clock the same evening, and as the weather was propitious, the passengers were congratulating themselves on having so fair prospects of a prompt arrival. The captain was a Virginian of the ante-bellum school, who, with true Southern laxity of discipline and a seeming immunity from disaster, often allowed his vessel to crash into docks and ground on sand spits, and as often escaped without any more serious results than delay. So it was generally understood that if we escaped the simple detentions often occurring, we would arrive on time, and the indications seemed favorable for us to do so. But, alas for human expectations when traveling by the Puget Sound steamers! About four o'clock we stopped at a little port called Argyle, and as we came near to the wharf, we saw that a trial of patience was at hand. A large pile of bales of hay, numerous crates of fowls and about fifty hogs with their feet bound were already on the wharf, and a man whose progression was barely perceptible was wheeling sacks of potatoes on a barrow from a warehouse at the beginning of the long wharf to the steamer for shipment. Perplexed anxiety was visible on almost every face in a moment.

"They'll never get all that freight on, with the load we already have," said one.

"They won't have a chance to put the potatoes on before morning," said another, as he observed the snail-like movements of the man at the barrow; and impatience was deepening into downright anger as the last bale, and crate and sack was finally stowed away.

"Come, boys, slide these fellows on in a hurry, now," said the captain, casting a look toward the fettered animals.

"They've all got to be weighed, yet," deliberately and unemotionally remarked one of the men on the wharf, as he thrust his hand into his pocket and drew out a large piece of tobacco, from which he proceeded to renew his quid.

The expressions that followed need not be recorded. It is sufficient to say that the crew set to work in high heat and disgust, a part being given the task of dragging the luckless porkers on the scales, which stood on the wharf, and the rest, that of sliding them down the plank into the hold. But a change was to come over the spirit of that (waking) dream. So long as the poor piggies were undisturbed, they remained discreetly silent; but the moment hands were laid on them, shrieks of all dimensions, qualities and cadences rent the air. From the profoundest bass to the most ear-splitting soprano, it was kept up until, overpowered by the uniqueness of the music, and, also, the impressiveness of the strains, the men forgot their ill humor in shouts of laughter, and everybody became resigned to the situation. Even the Indian woman's gravity broke down under the novel strain, and she joined the rest. Recovering from a paroxysm of laughter into which I had fallen when first overcome by the extravaganza to which we were being treated, I naturally turned towards my dusky sister, and was astonished to find her truly Indian mouth stretched literally from ear to ear and tears of delight starting from her shining eyes. At last the depths of her immobile nature had been reached. It was sundown before we finally steamed out into the channel again, but nobody grumbled.

Coupeville, on Whidby Island, is reached from Port Townsend. by, first, a small ferryboat, which runs as close to the beach as possible, then a row boat through the surf, and then a stage across the island ; but when I arrived, I found there some of the brightest and most enterprising W. C. T. U. women of Washington. Making a very small beginning, they had fought their way up against a determined foe to recognition and independence, being accepted leaders in all moral work and having headquarters of their own. As I held a meeting there on Sunday night and was due at La Conner on Monday, I was obliged to rise at two o'clock in the morning to catch the boat for that place. Being escorted to the wharf, and having escaped mishap from darkness and slippery gangplanks and finally got on board the steamer, I thought my trials for the day were over, but again

I had not calculated on the uncertainty of Puget Sound travel. About nine o'clock the steamer stopped in the open water, and I was told that I must make the rest of the trip in a row-boat, with four other passengers. A light rain was falling, and as the distance was estimated at from five to fifteen miles, the outlook was not promising. But we took our seats in silence, endeavoring to make the best of an unpleasant matter, and as there was water above and below us and our boat proved to be leaky, it may be appropiate to say that we went on swimmingly for the first hour or more. Then we stopped.

"What's wrong?" asked a young artist who was sitting beside me.

"Nothing, only the bottom is a little too near the top," answered the mate.

And such proved to be the case. We had grounded several miles from our destination, and that, with a swiftly receding tide. The oarsmen strained and tugged and finally thrust their oars into the yielding mud in an attempt to shove the boat off, but all in vain. As if in sympathy with the misery of the situation the clouds increased their dripping to a heavy down-pour, and the water that did not remain in the garments of those unprovided with storm coats ran down and added to the four or five inches already in the bottom of the boat. The nearest land was about a half mile distant, and towards it all looked with longing eyes.

"If we could get there and build a fire, it would be an improvement on this," said the artist; but as the dimensions of the "if" were painfully visible, his remark passed unheeded.

It did not take the mate long to decide that the boat could not be moved by ordinary means, and nodding a silent command to the oarsmen, he began unlacing his shoes, which example the two men followed. Divesting themselves of shoes and stockings and rolling their pantaloons above their knees, they stepped boldly out into the chilling water. Such a course seemed simply suicidal, particularly with regard to the oarsmen, who were reeking with perspiration from their long row and unusual efforts, but as there was no alternative to offer, I concluded it was a time when silence would be the better part of mercy, and said nothing. The men succeeded in shoving the boat off, but as our chance of escaping a seven hours' wait for high tide lay in our reaching the deep channel flowing at the base of the bluff before us, we were not yet out of danger of losing our lives from exposure or the upsetting of the boat on the treacherous rocks around us. Twice again we made the attempt to reach the channel, and as many times grounded and were shoved off by the wading crew; but a detour of several miles was at last decided on, and we finally gained the safe water—not, however, until both oarsmen had failed at their task from chill and exhaustion, and the passengers had risen to the emergency, two taking the oars and one bailing the water from the boat.

The remaining distance was soon passed over, and we landed among the rocks at the foot of the steep bank at La Conner, the tide being at its lowest ebb, very thankful that matters were no worse. Looking up the discouraging acclivity, which was thickly strewn with rocks slippery with sea slime, I saw a gentleman about midway from the top holding a closed umbrella towards me as an aid to my ascent, and heard him asking, with strong Scotch accent, if I had really arrived. Assuring him that I certainly had, and was very glad to know somebody was there to meet me, I climbed up, and learned that the gentleman was Rev. John M. Baxter, pastor of the M. E. Church at La Conner, but only a short time from South America. He took me at once to his home, where his helpful wife made me welcome. After calling on the president of the Union, who was ill at the time, and holding a public meeting the same evening, I found a night's rest quite enjoyable, having been forty hours with but two hours' sleep.

Tuesday morning came in with a cloudless sky, warm sunshine following, and as Rev. Baxter was to convey me to Bayview, nine miles distant, we felt that the day had been fitted to our needs. We started about nine o'clock, and, excepting that the road for the greater part of the distance ran through—literally through a sort of blue clay, which was said to be rich in aluminum, and into which metal we had occasion to sincerely wish it had been transmuted before we set out upon it, the ride was a most enjoyable one. Although it was November, the air was as balmy as that of May in the eastern states, and birds of generous growth and beautiful colors sang sweetly in the wild rose bushes and dry sedge grass as we passed along. The country between La Conner and Bayview has been settled many years and, unlike most other parts, is very level, having been claimed from the waters by being dyked in. Its appearance would bring delight to the heart of a Hollander, and is a novel sight to those who never saw canals taking the place of roads.

Judging from the name, La Conner, that the section had originally been settled by French navigators, or that a mission conducted by a French priest had once existed there, I inquired if either was the case and was surprised by the information that the name, or, at least, a part of it, came originally from Ireland and not from France. As the story ran, one Mr. Connor, whose christened title I do not recall, had a wife named Lucy A., and together they had worked to make a home in the wilds, chosing to battle with the tides rather than the giant firs farther inland. As time went on, they saw the waters recede and the dry land appear in answer to their efforts, and as dykes were pushed forward, the acres increased until Mr. Connor and his wife Lucy A. became joint owners of sufficient land to entitle them to recognition as entities by, at least, a subdivision of that great caravan called "the people." Whether this subdivision recognized Mr. and Mrs. Connor as individual entities, and not as one combined entity bearing the name of Mr. Connor, with a full understanding of what it was doing, or whether it had been so long separated from the main caravan that it did not know that such things were "unpopular" with the main body, I do not know; but the fact that it did so recognize them is beyond question. Mr. Connor coincided with the people in the idea that his wife was an individual entity, and when, finally, it became necessary to formally christen the Connor boat landing, the only question that arose was the one as to which entity should receive the honor of being passed into history on the tongues of the people. After due deliberation, it was decided that, as towns were not supposed to need "front" names nor initials, there must be a combination of the joint cognomen with the christened name of the entity chosen, and just there came in the matter of euphony. Had it not been for euphony,

I fear that the whole matter of the unusual recognition would have gone for naught and the precedent thus established would have been lost sight of. It would not do to overtax the tongues that were to do the passing into history, and so it was decided that the combination proving to be the more euphonious should be the one for historical honors. After that point had been reached, but little time was necessary in which to arrive at the conclusion that "L. A. Connor" robbed of its abbreviating points and "struck down to lower case" in its second letter, would be much more euphonious than "WConnor" or "JConnor," or even "Billconnor" or "Johnconnor." The "e" was, probably, substituted to rob the name of its last Emeraldic appearance.

As the substance of the foregoing story was caught piecemeal by a mind somewhat distracted by frequent interludes of conversation on such subjects as oyster culture, oat crops, saw-mill sites and the merits of soft shell over hard shell clams, the reader is requested not to accept it as absolutely correct in every particular. In fact, it is barely possible that were it to be submitted to those most interested, some radical changes might be suggested. But the fact remains that the sunny little spot raised above the tide flats in Skagit county, Washington, and called La Conner, was named thus in honor of Mrs. L. A. Connor, who still lives in the neighborhood and whose residence I passed, much regretting that my limit of time would not permit me to interview its mistress.

Bayview is on a bluff overlooking long stretches of tide flats, with deep water in the distance. Doubtless, the present site of the town will be a point of future outlook on a busy scene below, where, with water dyked out and present clam-beds turned into building lots, the business of the place will be done. At the time of my visit the Bayviewers were hopefully scanning harbor appropriation lists, but, with such energetic, moral people in the town as the Elliots, with whom I stopped, churches and schools and general civilization will go on whether the Government does its duty or not.

After Bayview came Avon, on the Skagit River. To reach Avon, I was obliged to retrace my journey of the day before for two miles and wait in the open air more than an hour for the cars, which were but just beginning to make trips over a new strip of railroad running from Sedro, in the Skagit River country, to Anacortes, but a few miles from Bayview. Finally the train arrived, and after a short ride over an extremely rough track, we stopped beside an uncovered platform in the midst of a tract of fallen trees which covered the ground to a depth of ten feet or more in places, and were told that we had arrived at

Avon station. The town was a mile or more from the station through the rough clearing and unbroken forest, and the passengers were taken over in one of the ordinary, wide-tired, heavy Western farm wagons, drawn by two powerful Clydesdales. Where clearing had been attempted, the ponderous stumps had been blown out with dynamite, leaving yawning cavities into and out of which the team plunged and climbed alternately, the wagon often sinking to the hubs in the yielding earth. Avon is directly on the bank of the Skagit River, which is crossed by means of a rope ferry at that point for Mount Vernon, about two miles away on the opposite shore. Soon after arriving, the light showers that had been falling settled into a steady rain, which continued through the night, leaving no opportunity for observation further than that the river was too shallow at that point for any but very light draft vessels except during high water.

Going back to the station in the morning, I took the train for Anacortes, which is on Fidalgo Island and is a harbor for deep water vessels. Fidalgo Island is separated from the mainland only by shallow water, which barrier to access has been overcome by piling, and the railroad terminates at one of the three wharfs already built at Anacortes at the time of my visit.

Having at different times during my peregrinations had my attention attracted to various misleading inscriptions, such as "Board of Trade," "The Little Church," "Foreign Exchange" and the like, over saloon doors, I had concluded the liquor dealers had exhausted ingenuity in that direction; but upon going up to the hotel where I was to stop, I found that alcoholic brains were, as usual, far behind the unvitiated article. As I stepped out of the carriage, I saw the words, "No Bar Hotel," in large letters across the front of the building, and as that happy combination of originality and unequivocalness met my gaze, I felt that "our folks" were still at the head. Consequently I received a favorable impression of Anacortes at the outset, which was verified during my stay. The proprietor and his wife, Mr. and Mrs. Haggard, who had so fearlessly hung out their banner, and whom I found to be young people, told me that, quite contrary to what had been predicted, the enterprise of keeping a hotel without a liquor-selling annex of any kind had proved highly successful; and judging from the overfullness of the house, there could be no doubt that such was the case. As I rode through the town with Mrs. Haggard, who kindly insisted on my seeing all the sights, I was more and more delighted with the place, and also more and more impressed that, with its long stretch of accessible water front; its dry and sightly locations for building, and the fact that the productive country through which I had passed since leaving La

Conner lay contiguous, it could hardly fail to reach a state of permanent prosperity within a very few years. Like La Conner, Anacortes was named in honor of a woman, Mrs. Anna Cortes, whose name, like that of the island, would indicate a first settlement from Spain, but whom I did not have the opportunity to inquire in regard to.

CHAPTER VII.

The exposure while on my way to La Conner, together with the other discomforts incident to the filling of five appointments in as many consecutive days under such circumstances, brought on extreme hoarseness at Anacortes, and I was obliged to return to Port Townsend for a short rest. Returning to the work in the Bellingham Bay towns a week afterwards, the first point visited was Fairhaven, which name, unlike some previously mentioned, I found to be entirely appropriate. As the appointment had been requested for Sunday evening, I took the steamer on Saturday, arriving in Fairhaven about two o'clock in the afternoon only to find no arrangements as yet made, on account of faulty management of the mails. Just here it may not be out of place to say that over a good part of the far northwestern country, the postal service seems to be conducted more with a desire to give paying offices and contracts to favorites, without regard to honesty or responsibility, than to serve the public faithfully. The fact that a letter mailed at Port

Townsend the Saturday before was not received at Fairhaven until the day of my arrival, and that, with a mail boat running daily between the places, is but one of the minor instances of gross neglect of duty that came under my notice. There were some arrests made in the Port Townsend office soon after I finally left that place, but a general and thorough investigation of the mail service of the entire Northwest would be the only effective remedy.

Finding a remarkable amount of ignorance existing among the hackmen as to the residence of any of the W. C. T. U. officials, I took a carriage to the M. E. parsonage and found that the hackmen were not alone in either their ignorance or apathy regarding temperance work.

Having had some experiences in such emergencies, I asked, without further waste of time, "Who is the most influential woman you have here?" feeling quite sure that in her I would find a white ribboner.

"Mrs. Judge Kellogg is the woman," said the driver, without hesitation; and to Mrs. Judge Kellogg's I told him to drive me.

On reaching Mrs. Kellogg's residence I found my conjectures were not only correct, but that she was the local president's mother, and would assume all responsibility for the time being.

Then Western energy was brought to bear, and the original plan was carried out. On Monday, Mrs. Kellogg drove me within view of Happy Valley, which is a sunny little dale a mile or so from Fairhaven, towards which the town is fast extending. At no other place on Bellingham Bay did I find such magnificent water views as are had from the heights at Fairhaven.

Sehome and Whatcom, which lay so near together that steps were being taken for their consolidation, and which are but a few miles from Fairhaven, were my next points, and on Monday afternoon I took the ferry-boat for the first named place. Upon consultation with Mrs. K. G. C. Graves, of Sehome, and Rev. T. J. Massey, of Whatcom, I found it would be necessary for me to remain in the two places a week, which afforded me some opportunity for observation.

In Sehome I found Mrs. Elizabeth Lyle Saxton, the well-known suffragist, who had but recently sought the haunts of civilization after a long rest in the forest from public work, and heard from her the story of her "taking up a claim." Having for some time been suffering from the weariness brought by too much publicity —the sense of "never being at home" that comes to every public speaker, Mrs. Saxton concluded to retire, with her youngest son, to a "lodge in the vast wilderness" of Puget Sound firs for a length of time that shoud be determined by experience. Going out about twelve miles from Sehome, she pre-empted a hundred and sixty acres of land, had a cabin erected and set up housekeeping in true pioneer style, her son bringing supplies from the town by such chance opportunities as an occasional settler's wagon offered, and "packing" them over the distance that the wagons did not reach. Quite in keeping with her ability in public work, she "held down" her claim till the necessary time expired, and soon sold it at a profit of about one thousand dollars. For the enlightenment of those who do not understand the process by which land is secured from the Government in the western country, I will explain that there is a vast difference between "taking up" and "holding down" a claim. The first is very easy, but the last is what tries men's—and women's—souls. To "take up" a claim, one has only to go to the land office and pay a few dollars for the filing of the claim, at the same time stating that it is the intention to make the required improvements; but the "holding down" is to brave solitude and dangers, from the elements, wild beasts, reptiles, etc.; to do without luxuries and put forth a good deal of physical effort, and to lose touch with the world generally for a period of from six months to five years, according to the particular kind of claim chosen. The pre-emption clause of the land law, which required but a six months' residence on the land before purchase has, however, been repealed recently, I believe.

"How did you enjoy your experience?" I asked Mrs. Saxton.

"I would not have missed it for anything! I look back on that year with regret that it is past, and nothing but the fact that my boy must be educated ever induced me to return to town life," was her answer.

And, indeed, there is an enchantment about the peculiar wildness of the extreme northwestern forests that is almost irresistible to the true lover of nature.

Whatcom, although built largely on piles, over tide flats, so far as regards its business portion, and lacking the natural harbor of both Sehome and Fairhaven, has already absorbed the former, and will, doubtless, take in the latter within a few years. Being nothing but a wilderness two years before my visit, it had grown into a city of eight thousand inhabitants, and the dynamiting of elephantine stumps and piling of mud flats was still going on, while every steamer deposited on its wharves newcomers, with their travel-stained boxes, bags and bundles.

On the Monday morning following my arrival at Sehome, I arose at an early hour in order to reach the boat for Blaine, away up on the Gulf of Georgia, close to the British Columbia line, and was escorted to the wharf just at dawn. But I did not go to Blaine that day. After walking the entire length of the half mile of wharf, there being no carriages at that hour, I was told that there might be a boat going to Blaine that day, and there might not. I soon learned that the regular steamer had been disabled, and the only possibility of reaching Blaine by water would be by some chance boat that might be going that way.

"Why can't you go by the train?" finally asked one of the wharfmen who had been obliged to seek shelter in the wharf house from the torrents of rain that began to fall.

Knowing that a railroad was being built through to New Westminster, in British Columbia, I caught eagerly at the suggestion, and asked if trains were really running. The man said they were, on each alternate day, and that he was certain Monday was one of the days on which trains ran.

Happy thought! I could take a car ride, after so much water travel.

Yet, I did not go to Blaine that day. I inquired for the depot, and was told there was none as yet, but that by standing on the wharf where the railroad track crossed it, I could signal the train and it would stop.

"When will the train start?" I asked.

"'Bout one or two o'clock they gen'ly come along," the man answered.

The delightful uncertainty as to which of the hours mentioned would prove to be the right one was lost sight of in the thought that I must leave the wharf and avoid further exposure till the first, at least, of the hours should arrive; and as a carriage soon came out with passengers for the Seattle steamer, I secured a seat and returned to the town.

Going again to the wharf soon after noon, I inquired if anything definite was known of the time of the train's arrival, and finally a man was brought to me who said there would be no train that day.

"What is the trouble?" I asked.

"That blamed devil's bread pan is r'arin' up again," was the answer.

I do not recall just what my first expression was after that remarkable piece of information, but am inclined to the idea that it was a somewhat severe, "Sir?" It took the form of an interrogation, I am certain, and the man at once proceeded to explain that in building the road, the men had found a spot of some dimensions where the earth had so settled under the track as to require a great amount of filling, and then, from some unknown cause at an unknown depth, had risen up again; and that that tidal process had been going on till so suggestive of diabolical aid that the spot had been christened, "The Devil's Bread Pan."

Then I did not want to go to Blaine, by rail, neither on that nor any other day—at least, until the spirit that presided over the "bread pan" should have been exorcised.

The next morning, I found two steamers, the Sehome and Mountaineer, lying at the dock awaiting passengers for Blaine; the first being a good-sized passenger boat that made regular trips three times a week, and the last being a diminutive "independent." Having had some nerve-trying experience with the jarring, grating motion of the larger vessel, I took passage on the smaller, which flitted over the water like a bird and kept the passengers in a high state of merriment by a whistle that, beginning harmoniously, ended in a wail of so many startling variations as to suggest the last throes of some dying monster. I was afterwards told that the Mountaineer's owner had invented the whistle for purposes best known to himself, but that its sound never failed to overcome the gravity of all who heard it, whatever the original object might have been.

The town of Blaine lies upon a more level surface than either of the three towns I had just visited, and consequently is possessed of a less number of commanding points of view; but as it is surrounded with snow-clad peaks, there is no lack of scenery. Although the middle of December was near at hand, the air was comfortably warm, and the pleasing aspect of the place was marred by nothing but its extremely muddy streets. Nearly all of the main streets of the towns in the Sound country are made of heavy planks, resting on sills sometimes placed on the earth's surface, but often on piles at a distance anywhere from one to twenty-five feet above. As Blaine's "boom" had begun to subside before its streets had been planked, the latter were in a most sorry condition; as all the unplanked roads are in that country during the rainy season.

It was my intention to proceed on to New Westminster and Vancouver, in British Columbia, but upon inquiring at what hour the stage would start for the former place, I was told that it had been discontinued on account of the state of the roads. Finding that about six miles of almost bottomless mud would have to be forded to reach New Westminster, and an exhorbitant price placed on the undertaking, I concluded to return to Port Townsend and make preparation for my southward journey towards Oregon, leaving British Columbia towns for a time in the future when I should make the outer of the two loop trips to the

Pacific, going out by the most southern line of railroad and returning by the British Columbia route.

Port Townsend, though maligned, and sneered at and ignored by rival towns of later birth, is, without doubt, the most charming place for residence purposes in the entire Puget Sound country on the United States shore. The main business portion of the town is still where the first settlement began, on a narrow bench of land just above the reach of the tides, and back of which rises a high bluff. The bluff, which is now easily mounted by means of an electric car line, was formerly climbed by rude stairways, two of which were still in use when I was last in the place. But even those who climb the stairs are fully repaid by the view that lies before them on reaching the summit. The churches, school buildings and by far the greater number of private residences are on the higher level, and consequently, a person visiting only the water front would have no correct idea of the city's extent or beauty. Although all nationalities are represented in Port Townsend, and Chinamen are almost as plentiful as the crows at Dungenness, I was set down on its wharves and traversed its streets alone at midnight again and again without molestation or any thought of fear.

During the entire time from the middle of October until the first of January there was but one week of storm sufficient to interfere with travel, and not more than a half dozen all day fogs at Port Townsend. There came on a heavy windstorm about the eighteenth of December, lasting five days, during which time I could not leave the city, either by water or land, but the experience it brought was well worth the delay. Wishing to go to Roche Harbor, on San Juan Island, I went twice to the wharf and as many times returned again, awed by the force of the storm. Finally I concluded to take a train on Port Townsend's only railroad and explore the Hood's Canal region; but my explorations in that section were never made. The Port Townsend Southern R. R. is, or was at that time, but a short line of unfinished railroad running from Port Townsend in the direction of Olympia, but terminating in the Hood's Canal country, much short of that place. Hood's Canal is one of the longer and larger of the many canal-like bayous reaching out from the different bays and inlets on the coast and usually called sloughs, and it strikes off into the forest south of Port Townsend. The Port Townsend Southern Depot is a couple of miles from the central part of the city, on the water front, and is reached by the street car line. So, with storm coat, hand-bag and umbrella, I took a car for the depot, fully determined that if I could not get out of the city by water, I would do so by land. But

I had not taken into consideration the fact that a railroad might be built in the water. As the street-car stopped at the terminus near the depot, and a good distance from the water, we found the spray beating clear up to the track, but, nothing daunted, set out to reach the depot platform. That proved to be a feat that could only be accomplished by joining hands and submitting to be led by such of the gentlemen as were able to make their way against the wind. Reaching the shelter of the building, we recovered our breath and at once got upon the train, which was ready for departure. The track was built over the water, on piles, for a considerable distance, and as there was some doubt about its safety, considering the strain to which it had been subjected since the storm came on, it was thought best to place the engine at the rear of the train, on account of its great weight, and push the passenger cars out to test the track. That arrangement seemed highly satisfactory to the trainsmen, but was not altogether pleasing to the passengers. Yet little was said, and soon the train began to move slowly out. To the left, the view was one of tumultuous water, with a small sloop flying a signal of distress and rearing and plunging as if endowed with life, as she dragged her anchors and drifted on to certain destruction if not succored in time; while to the right was a high bluff, around which the train must make its way before reaching a place of safety. After proceeding a short distance, the train stopped, and several men were sent forward to repair the track where the waves were running over it ; and for just an hour and forty-five minutes by my watch, we waited there, with the spray beating over the tops of the cars, and the gallant wrecking crew clinging to the rails ahead of us, as they pried and wedged, in a vain attempt to repair the damage wrought by the beating of heavy drift logs against the track. But the limit of endurance was finally reached, and as the chilled and dripping men climbed back upon the cars, the general feeling was that any further effort would be but a tempting of Providence. So the train drew back to the station and all returned to the city.

CHAPTER VIII.

Two days after my vain attempt to explore the Hood's Canal region, I made a tempestuous voyage to Roche Harbor, but, happily enjoying a general exemption from sea-sickness, found it no unpleasant experience. All the other passengers were soon prostrated, and when, after nightfall, we finally arrived, it was a dejected company that landed and proceeded to the Hotel de Haro, the one public house in the place. Knowing that alluring titles were often accompanied with meagre ideas of the needs of guests, no picture of comfort flitted before my mind as I groped my way in the darkness towards the hotel, and, consequently, an agreeable surprise awaited me. Being ushered into a large sitting-room fully furnished in modern style, where a broad fire-place was piled high with logs, we were all spell-bound for a moment by the contrast to the dirty, ill-smelling steamer. But my surprise was still greater when I went into the dining-room and found a table superior to those of many so-called first class hotels in the large cities. The mystery was explained when I learned that the proprietor was Mr. McMillen, president of the Roche Harbor Lime Co., and through whose courtesy my appointment had been made.

No one unfamiliar with the crudeness of hotel-keeping in the newer sections of the West can form an adequate idea of the genuine thankfulness with which a home-like place, with clean beds and good food, is hailed by travelers in that country. That the lack of home comforts and cheer is one of the greatest sources of intemperance in the West, there can be no doubt; and those who keep public houses where temperance, morality and good housekeeping reign, are doing a greater evangelistic work than the clergy can possibly do; for the reason that the first are ministering to a constant and everchanging concourse through many senses, while the last can reach but a limited number of people once a week through but one sense.

Soon after reaching the hotel, Rev. Dr. Dillon, one of the fathers of Methodism on the coast, arrived, having been a passenger on the East Sound steamer, which had been obliged to land its passengers at Roche Harbor on account of the storm. Having met Dr. Dillon when at Sehome, we were not strangers, and as he could not get passage to East Sound before Monday—it then being Friday

—he made an agreeable addition to our company over Saturday and Sunday.

There being no boat for Port Townsend before Tuesday, I was obliged to remain over Monday, and was given the choice of a yacht ride to Henry Island, one of the smaller islands a few miles distant, or a visit to the extensive lime works in the interest of which the small town has grown into existence. Choosing the former, I had a most enjoyable sail, after which, Mrs. McMillen showed me her roses, yet blooming in the garden, although Christmas was but two days away.

With a longing look towards the still unexplored islands of the Achipelago de Haro, I stepped on board the steamer Evangel, (the same on which I had journeyed from East Sound), with a feeling similar to that experienced on leaving a summer resort when the season is over and the attractions gone. But there was yet one more novel experience awaiting me. The storm had settled into perfect calm, and having taken on little freight except a few crates of fowls and a much-frightened cow, the steamer was gliding over the water at an encouraging rate and the passengers were in high good humor in the belief that the Evangel would redeem herself from her record of mishaps and arrive at her dock before the street cars had ceased running and the hackmen had deserted the wharf in despair. Wednesday was to be spent in preparing for Christmas festivities, but we were soon reminded of the command to "take no thought for the morrow." At Lopez Harbor a short curve had to be made around the end of a sand spit to reach the wharf, but, with the usual heedlessness, the boat's prow was kept straight on to shore, and in a moment's time a shock and a quiver told us we were aground.

"Everybody go aft!" shouted the mate.

Everybody went aft with alacrity, but the tide was ebbing swiftly and so much time was lost by the apathy of the crew that all attempts to release the vessel were fruitless. It was then five o'clock, and the tide would not turn for two hours. Knowing that an eight hours' wait was before me, I went ashore in a small boat and joined Mrs. Johnson, who, having espied me when the steamer grounded, was awaiting my coming. A good-sized vessel left high and dry as the tide receded was too novel a sight to be lost, and immediately after supper we repaired to the beach. As the tide fell low, the discovery was made that the steamer's keel had thrown up furrows of clams on each side as it plowed into the beach, and immediately the sailors concluded to add clam chowder to their Christmas bill of fare. Sacks and buckets were hunted up and a hilarious harvesting began. As the water receded, the steamer listed more and more till at last it stood at an angle that suggested its having retired for the night, and which rendered the situation of those on board rather embarrassing.

"Why, you can't stand up, and there is no place to lie down ; and as for settin', my wife's been slanted up agin the table till she can't hardly stir," said a San Juan Islander who crept down the steep gang plank about eleven o'clock, and who had solemnly informed me when the mishap occurred, that it was the last time he would ever travel by *water* with "weemen folks" in charge ; seeming entirely unmindful of the fact that he lived on an island.

Catching a couple of hours' rest on a sofa at my friend's house, I arose at two o'clock in the morning, and going to the wharf, found the steamer ready for departure. To save the trouble of placing a plank to the upper deck, the mate insisted on our reaching the cabin by passing through the hold, and led the way through a catacomb-like passage, where we barely escaped the heels of the long suffering cow. Being immediately behind the mate, who carried a lantern, I caught a lightning-like flash of a pair of hoofs, and utter darkness followed. The cow, evidently having concluded that the inventors of inclined planes for her to stand on would be guilty of any iniquity, had assumed the defensive and kicked the lantern into many pieces. Fearing a repetition of that evidence of displeasure, our procession came to a stand-still, and while the mate was hunting for a match, I informed Bossy that I was quite in sympathy with her mood, but implored her to be less demonstrative. She may not have understood my remarks, and she may have exhausted her ill humor in that one fell blow ; but having interceded for her before going ashore and had her fastenings lengthened to enable her to make the most of her uncomfortable quarters, I shall always think it was true gratitude that caused her to desist and allow us to proceed in safety.

Leaving Port Townsend for Seattle two days before New Year's, I remained in the latter place two weeks, during which time more or less rain fell every day. Having letters of introduction to Mrs. C. K. Jenner, Mr. D. T. Denny and others of the earlier residents, I soon learned of the brave struggles that had been made to keep spirituality abreast with temporal matters in the wild onsweep of the city's progress, and found that the cowardly act of robbing the Washington women of the ballot had proved the most effective blow to morality the town had ever experienced. No longer having any faith in men who cravenly turned on their own mothers, wives and daughters and struck down their liberty and usefulness at the behest of the liquor power, many of the more influential and wealthy ladies were standing aloof from the interests of the city in disgust, and indecision as to what could be done, while the tide of "all uncleanness" swept up to their doors and left its tribute of misery and want. All power being thrown back into the hands of men, self-interest had found its way into the fold of moral workers, and, while the people over the state were giving generously to the support of a temperance newspaper and the machinery of a state temperance alliance having their headquarters at Seattle, no results were to be seen except a worthless sheet, which died while I was in the city, and a few fat salaries. The Y. M. C. A., assisted by the ladies of the city, held a reception on New Year's, which I attended in company with Mrs. Harriet Parkhurst, State W. C. T. U. Superintendent of Jail and Prison Work, and which furnished a pleasant contrast to the sights of fallen manhood to be seen on the streets.

After visiting Ballard, eight miles from Seattle, I took the steamer for Tacoma, but finding no arrangements made for either public or society meetings, proceeded on to Steilacoom, where the older of the two state lunatic asylums is located, and which is one of the oldest towns on the Sound. There I found a genuine W. C. T. U. welcome awaiting me, owing to the efficiency of the local president, Mrs. A. L. Bell, who added to her hospitality the courtesy of a drive to the Asylum, the one place of interest to strangers aside from the water view, which is one of great loveliness. The Asylum buildings are, as I understood, those of an old garrison of the earlier days, and are in no way pretentious; but the natural advantages for the restoration of the reason quite overbalanced all shortcomings in architecture. Although not large, the main building seemed sufficiently capacious for the number of inmates, and apparently was very well conducted; but the barracks formerly occupied by the soldiers were used as dormitories for some of the male inmates, and, in the absence of any heating apparatus, must have been uncomfortable from dampness during the winter season. There was, I noticed, an absence of restraints, such as strait-jackets, muffs, strapping-chairs, etc., that gave evidence of the superintendent's knowledge of the important fact in the care of the insane, that the greater the liberty given an insane person, within the limit of safety to himself and others, the greater are his chances of recovery.

Going from Steilacoom to Olympia, I was at last at the extreme southern point of Puget Sound and in the state capital. But why Olympia is the state capital, is a question no woman can answer, and is only one of the many "whys" that are constantly on the lips of strangers who visit the town. "Why don't they pave the streets?" "Why don't they have street cars that are not a disgrace to the town?" "Why are not the residents compelled to build sidewalks" are some of the questions heard; and one that often is and oftener might be asked during the session of the legislature is, "Why do the people trust the interests of a great state to the hands of men quite unworthy of ordinary respect?" A disgraceful fight occurred between legislators in the principal hotel while I was in Olympia, and during my four days sojourn I several times witnessed groups of the honorable (?) representatives of the people congregated at saloon doors in a state of garrulous intoxication. The disreputable element was so much in the majority that the only wonder was that the reputable members did not go home in disgust and escape such enforced companionship.

Yet, instead of standing shoulder to shoulder in harmonious effort against such outside influences, the Olympians had weakened their own moral force by sectarian discord; and wrangles over the Trinity, which no mortal has yet claimed to fully understand, had well-nigh obscured Christ and his teachings, whether divine or human. The recent revival of religious services by the Unitarians after an interval of some years of silence had been the signal for a renewal of almost forgotten hostilities, and the too frequent spectacle of so-called religious zeal appearing in the form of unreasoning persecution was likely to be repeated. But, calling on the pastors and their wives in the interest of the W. C. T. U., the usefulness of which had been lost some years before in the conflict of creeds, I found them largely in favor of harmony, and I finally left Olympia with the pleasing conviction that Superstition's cruel head was receiving a blow from this century's intelligence that would restore the birthright of kindness to the people of the next.

I had reached the end of water travel at Olympia, and from there went southward by rail, stopping at Tumwater, from which place I visited South Union with Rev. G. F. Mead, of the M. E. church, who had a charge there. South Union is several miles from the railroad, in the midst of the hop-raising district, and I there saw something of the struggle against the temptation to raise hops for the brewers, rather than grow cereals, fruits and vegetables. As usual, the women were waging a brave warfare against wrong, and the beer barrels seemed losing ground.

Returning to Tumwater, I proceeded on south to Bucoda, Chehalis, Centralia and Castle Rock, the last named place being my last stopping point in Washington for the time. The country from Bucoda to Castle Rock is much more level than the greater part of the Sound country, but has few attractions, apparently, further than its adaptation to farming purposes. Castle Rock is on the Cowlitz River, which is navigable from that point to the Columbia, but which has so strong a current that navigation is much easier down stream than up. The town itself is a sunny little hamlet with an air more of ease than neatness, but possessing some very intelligent and kind hearted people. A rather poor quality of coal, which has a dull appearance, unlike either the anthracite or bituminous coal of the East, is mined within sight of the town, and the good-natured inhabitants pay six dollars a ton for it, quite thankful that Washington produces coal of any quality.

"Oh," said Mrs. Michener, my hostess and one of the older residents, "we think that is low, and we are very proud to think our part of the state produces coal."

CHAPTER IX.

Arriving in Portland, Oregon, and finding the arrangements for my tour over the state yet unmade, I remained a week, the guest of Mrs. A. R. Riggs, State W. C. T. U. president, during which time I visited Vancouver, Washington, on the opposite side of the Columbia, where I met Mrs. M. L. T. Hidden, one of the most able W. C. T. U. women of Washington.

Portland, which is on the Willamette River but a short distance from its confluence with the Columbia and about seventy miles from Astoria, has the advantage over the Sound ports of being a fresh water harbor, which is a matter of some importance to navigators for several reasons, a not unimportant one being the fact that vessels often come into port with a great weight of barnacles attached to their hulls, which pests fresh water causes to release their hold and the vessels are thus relieved. While on my way to Seattle from Port Townsend, a gentleman engaged in the shipping interests spoke of a project for cutting a channel from the Sound at Seattle to Lake Washington, which is not far from the city, that vessels might run into fresh water, so great was the need.

The principal part of Portland is on the western bank of the Willamette, and rises gradually from the water's edge for a considerable distance, finally dotting the sides of steep hills, the summits of which form what are called Portland Heights. But the city extends over the river and takes in a large strip of the peninsula lying between the Willamette and Columbia. Until recently, all that part on the eastern bank of the Willamette was a separate corporation, and is still known as East Portland, although it has been annexed to the city proper. Taken all in all, Portland gives a more homelike feeling to an Eastern person than any other town of its dimensions in the Northwest, yet it possesses the novel feature of a Chinese Quarter in the very center of the city. Second street, which is the third street from the river running parallel with it, is occupied wholly by Chinese for several blocks, and other streets intersecting have a sprinkling, for greater or less distances, of the queer looking shops and quite as queer looking shop men. Yet, I never heard a complaint regarding the Chinese while in Portland, which I visited four times, remaining, in all, nearly two months, and I never had cause to fear in passing through either the

Chinese Quarter or the vicinity of the wharves at night, although I several times had occasion to do both.

February, March, April and a part of May were spent in Southern Oregon, my first stopping place being Cottage Grove, one hundred and forty-three miles south of Portland and at the extreme southern end of the Willamette Valley. On the morning of my departure for the southern part of the State, which was in the first days of February, I saw snow for the first time during the winter, the ground being barely covered as I walked to the street-car on Portland Heights.

As the train left the city and its suburbs behind, and we entered the famed Willamette Valley, I looked for the beautiful houses, good fences and general air of thrift I had pictured as belonging to a section so long settled, but saw instead, ancient and unclassified styles of architecture; few and ill kept fences; untrimmed fruit trees covered with moss, and a gloomy, hibernating aspect quite disastrous to my animated ideal, and, also, quite out of keeping with the mild weather. The larger towns presented a more modern and active appearance, but the farms and smaller stations all seemed touched with the wand of Decay. The growth of moss on everything added to the antiquated appearance, and turning to a countryman in a seat near mine, I asked if the trees in an orchard we were passing were alive.

"Yes, some of them are, but one or two more years will kill the last one, if they don't get the moss off," was the answer.

"Can it be removed?" I asked.

"Oh, yes; it can all be taken off with a little work," he said.

"Why is it not done?" I asked, in astonishment; having noticed many orchards in the same condition and concluded there was no remedy, or such would not be the case.

"Oh, you can't make a mossback work," he answered, evidently in some surprise at the question, and with a strong accent on the word "work."

Having heard Oregonians spoken of both as "mossbacks" and "webfeet," I asked if those titles applied to all alike.

"Not exactly—no ma'm," said he, apparently at a loss just how to explain the difference, but continued, "I suppose I'm a webfoot, but I'm not a mossback. It is mostly the ones that settled the country, that we call mossbacks. When they came, they were satisfied with enough to eat, and it didn't take much work to get that; and so they got into the habit of living that way, and they don't want to change—*and you can't make them*.

Beginning to understand the situation, I incidentally asked where the first settlers were from and received the answer, "From the South. A good many are from Missouri, but they are from all over the South."

Immediately a great light dawned on my puzzled brain. I understood at once why the unpretentious habitations, with their numerous "additions" and out-buildings, had seemed so familiar to my eyes. Southern ease and simplicity of taste, and the inclination to command but not work, born of and fostered by slavery, explained the whole matter of buildings, orchards, fences and the still more difficult one of the disinclination to change and the determination not to be compelled to do so. Later I was informed that when slavery was endeavoring to add to its territory, many Southerners were sent to California and Oregon in the hope to outvote the free state settlers, as was the case soon after with Kansas; and the records of the contest at the time of Oregon's admission as a state, verify the statement. Yet, there is quite another color to the history of many of those who followed a few years later, but are classed with the early settlers. While I was in the state, I learned the story of some of the Southern residents who went to Oregon in the early sixties, and although they had, through birth and education, been in the wrong in some instances, the sufferings that had been forced upon them would have embittered any but the best of minds. Living in free states or slave states bordering on them, and sympathizing with friends or relatives in the South, they had been hunted and persecuted by over-zealous patriots and loot-loving guerillas till they had crept to their wagons, often at night, and having no other way open before them, had turned their faces westward, with tears and misgivings, and for weary days, and weeks, and months they had journeyed on, climbing mountains, and traversing desolate sage brush plains, many times cold and hungry, and ill and suffering from thirst, and finally had reached the land "where rolls the Oregon," and been succored by their old-time associates. Children were born, and friends were buried on those dreary marches; and if those who lived through them are sensitive to the touch of rude hands on the wounds then received, rebuke is much out of place from those who never passed through such experiences.

The aspect presented to the eye by the Willamette Valley as one journeys southward is first that of a wide and level stretch of country dotted here and there with low, water-worn hills and not heavily wooded except near the river; and as progress is made, the outlook narrows and the level surface is oftener broken; the complete view giving the impression that the now modest Willamette was a mighty river covering many miles of country on each side of its present bed at a time not a great number of centuries in the past. The products of the valley are similar in kind and amount to those of the Middle States with the exception of corn, which, though raised for home consumption, never reaches the state of luxuriance seen east of the Rocky Mountains. Apples, pears, prunes and plums grow in great abundance, but a flaky, gray moss, perhaps more properly, lichen, of which mention has been made, is something of a pest to fruit growers. The moss-growing strip takes in the entire length of the Willamette Valley and extends to the farther end of the Umpqua Valley, which follows the Willamette on the south. The moss forms on young trees quite as readily as on old, and to a person unacquainted with the country, the shrub growth covering the hillsides has the appearance in winter of being clothed in delicate foliage.

At Cottage Grove I had the pleasure of meeting Mr. A. N. Beecher, who is a relative of the late Rev. Henry Ward Beecher and was mayor of Oberlin, Ohio, at the time of the "John Price rescue," in the old Abolition days. On a later visit, I was the guest of his daughter, Mrs. Anna M. Boldrick, and found the true Beecher spirit of opposition to wrong reproduced in her.

Continuing southward, I visited Drain, Oakland, Wilbur, Roseburg and Myrtle Creek, in the Umpqua Valley, which is more broken than the Willamette, but very beautiful to the sight, and also very productive. The weather being extremely wet, the mountain sides had become saturated, and landslides were of frequent occurrence; which fact I soon had forced upon my understanding by a blockade of the railroad track on both sides of the town of Myrtle Creek, at which place I was obliged to remain an extra day, not being able to either advance or retreat. For about fifty miles southward from Myrtle Creek the railroad runs through a most wild and chaotic country, which is a part of Southern Oregon's gold region; and about thirty miles of the road is a succession of tunnels, "cuts" and "fills" not well calculated for the enjoyment of nervous people, and certainly not successful in defying the element of water. Every year the rainy season detaches many tons of earth and rock, which bury the track and obstruct travel, and consequently, Cow Creek Canyon, as the section is called, is looked upon with dread by winter travelers acquainted with the route. Yet, through that country, my route to the towns in the extreme southern part of Oregon lay, and to go, or not to go, was the question. The non-arrival of my date list, which was to have reached me at Oakland,

and the assurance of residents and trainmen that more or less landslides and their attendant delay were sure to occur in the length of time necessary to reach all the points desired, decided the question in the negative, and I turned back, leaving the extreme southern towns for a future date. The train on which I left Myrtle Creek had been blockaded several times, the last delay being one of six hours, and the passengers were beginning to congratulate each other on their escape, when the train suddenly came to a stop and we were informed that the slide before us had "moved down." For more than two hours we waited and watched, as the dripping Chinamen shoveled earth and rolled the rocks away, presenting, in their peculiar garments, as they worked under the shadow of a high cliff in the deepening twilight, very much the appearance of an army of gigantic bats. The blockade finally being removed, we reached Oakland about ten o'clock at night, where I remained over two days, then continuing northward as far, as Albany, in Linn county, and visiting Cresswell, Eugene, Junction City, Harrisburg, Halsey, and Shedd, on the way.

When at Eugene, where the State University is located, it was my good fortune to be the guest of the family of Prof. Condon, State Geologist of Oregon, who has a very valuable geological collection, and one that throws great light on the primitive history of the entire Northwest. Evidences that a semi-tropical climate prevailed in the country at one time are numerous in the collection, and as Prof. Condon explained the significance of the location of each when found, I began to realize how absorbing such a "looking backward" might become.

CHAPTER X.

Coos county, which is on the Oregon coast at a point about one-third of the distance from Astoria to San Francisco, and which is reached by the ocean route at Coos Bay, is nearly inaccessible from the interior during the rainy season; yet it seemed necessary that I should reach that outlying field of W. C. T. U. work before the Pacific Coast W. C. T. U. Conference and Oregon W. C. T. U. Convention, which were to be held in Portland the last of May. Having been informed while at Drain that a stage line, operated when not closed by floods or landslides, ran into the Coos Bay country from that place, and being too far from Portland to take the ocean route, I concluded to return to the former place (Drain) and undertake the trip as soon as I should learn that the state of the roads would permit. But, to gain definite information regarding routes, distances, etc., is one of the trials of travel in the Northwest.

"There's no stage running from Drain, but there's one from Roseburg," said one man, who had "just been down there."

"They can't get through even on horseback from Roseburg now, but there's a stage running from Drain once a week," another assured me."

Going to the telegraph office, I learned that there was supposed to be a stage running from Drain to Scottsburg, thirty-six miles on the Coos county route, but was told, "It's ten chances to one that you can't get any farther."

Concluding to take the one chance, I arrived at Drain about two o'clock of an extremely wet morning, and upon inquiring of the landlord of the one hotel, was told that the route was open the entire distance to Marshfield, the principal town on Coos Bay, and that the stage left at six o'clock that morning.

Four hours' sleep, and a stage ride of thirty-six miles over a mountain road! The thought was appalling, but no time was to be lost, and I asked for a room.

"Haven't got such a thing. There isn't an empty bed in the house," the landlord answered, but suggested that I might get some rest on a lounge in the sitting-room.

Acting upon the suggestion, I succeeded in reaching a state of chill, damp misery quite unendurable by four o'clock, and passed the remaining two hours in physical culture and occasional *sotto voce* remarks on the peculiar tastes of a people who, though living in a tomb-like atmosphere, considered fire unnecessary. Probably no other one source of discomfort to an Eastern person in Oregon in the winter time is so great as lack of sufficient fire to overcome the dampness. By far the greater number of houses in the rural districts and smaller towns of Oregon are built entirely of wood, without plastering; the inside walls being of rough boards upon which common cotton sheeting is tacked as a surface for paper hanging; and as it is quite impossible to "break joints" sufficiently well in such walls to shut out the wind, drafts and dampness (also ill-fitting wall paper, which gives a look of dilapidation to the whole interior) are the results. Added to these is the fact that fire other than for the purpose of cooking is much more often conspicuous by its absence than its presence.

At six o'clock two vehicles, one a "buckboard" and the other a spring wagon, or, in Western parlance, a "hack," were driven up to the hotel, and, leaving my heavier baggage in care of the landlord, I took a seat in the latter conveyance, being confidentially and consolingly informed that they were both bad enough, but that I would be much more comfortable in the latter, as the former not only "slung mud" but always took the lead and, consequently, had to test the depth of "sinks" and "washouts;" while the one I would embark in was not likely to do anything worse than upset.

For the greater part of the distance from Drain to Scottsburg the road follows the Umpqua River, and in many places the track, which for miles is cut into the solid rock of a steep and high bluff, is forced so far out by the formation of the bank that but a few inches intervene between passing vehicles and abrupt descents of greater or less depth to the river below. For a distance of about two miles in one place on the route the descent is about two hundred feet, nearly perpendicular, to the water, while on the landward side the rocky cliff rises from ten to twenty-five feet so close that it may be reached by the hand in places as one rides past. Yet the higher portions of the road were much preferable to the lower except where the ascents were so steep as to be perilous to teams and passengers. In places near the level of the river, the wagons often sunk to the axles, and could only be taken through by the straining teams after being relieved of all the male passengers.

About midway between Drain and Scottsburg is Elkton, which is on Elk Creek and which is looked forward to with longing by all familiar with the route, and backward upon with regret by every traveler who passes that way. Yet, Elkton is not beautiful; neither are there gold or silver mines at Elkton. But there is a gem—possibly more, but certainly one—of great price at Elkton, and the gem is in the form of a woman who knows how to cook! A poor, low roofed building is the hotel at Elkton, but the table it sets is a delight to the palate, and the memory of its light, sweet bread, its perfectly cooked wild game and domestic fowls and its delicious, old-fashioned "preserves" comes to many a weary traveler who has found the task of digesting solid dough, unmasticable steaks and fermented fruit too absorbing to admit of sleep. The amount of food consumed by our party of eleven was something enormous, but the half dollars were handed over with such alacrity, and the cooking was praised so unstintingly that a much less pleasant host than ours would have been fully satisfied.

Soon after leaving Elkton we reached a point where a large landslide had occurred a short time before, and where it seemed that the very jarring of the wagons on the rocks must bring down another, which was being held in check by a few large pines that had sent their roots deep into the crevices of the primitive formation of the hillside and were literally holding the ground. Yet, we passed on in safety, and when darkness shut the dangers from our sight, two ladies in the first wagon began singing, and "Nearer My God to Thee," "Hold the Fort," "Rock of Ages" and many other familiar hymns rang out hopefully and drove away fear.

We arrived at Scottsburg soon after eight o'clock, having been fourteen hours on the way, and thirteen in actual motion, showing a rate of speed of a trifle less than three miles an hour. But the end was not yet for my fellow travelers. The route from Scottsburg was by way of the Umpqua River to the ocean, and as the small steamer running between could only make the trip at high tide, and only made three trips a week, the passengers must either rise at three o'clock the next morning or wait two days. Many of the men had walked fully half the distance just passed over, and as a consequence were in a worse state of exhaustion than the women; yet, little grumbling was heard.

A commercial traveler evidently unused to such heroic effort, but who had bravely "kept up with the procession," rubbed his stiffened limbs and gave vent to his feelings by the remark, "This is nothing less than murder!" but immediately desisted and joined in the laugh when a veteran comrade called out, "Don't kick now, when we've just got the cinch on 'em. They can't make us walk on the water."

Notification having been sent of my coming, my arrival was expected, and I was shown to the residence of Mrs. Ozouf, where I was to rest until the second coming of the steamer. Scottsburg is in a tiny valley shut in by towering hills, and, having no other means of ingress or egress than the ones mentioned, is not a place where one would look for wealth and ease; but as, weary and mud bespattered, I stepped into Mrs. Ozouf's sitting-room, I realized anew that the West was a country of surprises. Looking about me, I everywhere saw evidences of refinement, and soon learned that my host and hostess had but just returned from a trip to Europe. But the solution of the matter was simple. Many years before a young Frenchman had hired out to a tanner who had located on the Umpqua where the little group of houses called Scottsburg now stands, and who marketed his products in San Francisco. He worked and saved, then married and his wife worked with him until he was able to buy out his employer. After a time the couple became independent and arrived at the very sensible conclusion that they had worked long enough and would enjoy the proceeds of their labor.

Rising at about four o'clock the third morning after my arrival, I embarked for Gardiner, which is on the Umpqua nine miles from its mouth, and at which point large lumber mills are located.

There I passed Easter, finding a very intelligent body of women arrayed in defense of their homes, while a majority of the men had signed petitions for their destruction by the sale of liquor ; it being necessary in Oregon for saloon keepers to petition for license. From Gardiner, I was to make the entire trip to Marshfield without stop, and with helpful suggestions regarding wraps for protection against the sea breezes and many kind wishes from the white-ribbon sisters, I took the boat at seven o'clock on Tuesday morning for the ocean, where a twenty miles' stage trip on the ocean beach intervened between the mouth of the Umpqua and Coos Bay. The weather was fine, and as we drew near the mouth of the river, I went on deck to take my first view of the Pacific. A wide line of breakers sending spray to a great height, and a limitless stretch of blue water beyond met my gaze, and as a troop of thoughts struggled for mastery in my mind, I was brought back to my surroundings by the question, "Where's the wharf ?"

But, no wharf was to be seen, and while those new to the route were wondering where we were to make a landing, the steamer stopped in midstream and a yawl was lowered by which to transfer us to the shore.

"How are we to get in ?" was the next question, and for a few minutes that absorbed all minds.

The bottom of the yawl must have been fully five feet from the deck of the steamer, and as the latter possessed neither steps nor gang board, the problem of how to get in had to be solved as best it could be. Like many of the other difficult and quite unnecessary problems encountered in that country, it was solved by the passengers themselves, in one way and another, the captain making no effort towards assistance.

Two wagons were waiting on the beach near a small stable, which was the only sign of human handiwork on the lone shore for twenty miles. At low tide the ocean beach, over which we passed, furnishes an excellent track for wagons, the sand where wet being so solidly packed that the wheels make almost no indentation ; and over that natural highway stages have been running for fully twenty-five years, although in following that plan the owners of the line have constantly verified the saying, "Laziness always takes the most pains." To utilize the beach it is necessary to move with the tides, and that necessitates setting out at all hours of the night as well as of the day. Moreover, a road made through the timber a little inland would have the advantage of shelter and continual safety ; while, by the beach route, ocean storms must be breasted, and an accident to teams or vehicles while on the way usually necessitates a camp in the sand above high tide mark for many hours. Yet, such suggestions would be wholly lost on the owners of the transportation line from Drain to Marshfield. The roads have always been mended with fir brush, or "bresh," as the supervisor of roads between Drain and Scottsburg called it, the tides have always reached Scottsburg, and gone out on the beach, and no Oregonian of the "mossback" species can be made to see that any change is necessary.

Having the company of a young lady school teacher and her brother, and the bright sunshine making the day comfortably warm, I found the ride over the beach a delightful one, and on arriving at the landing opposite Empire City, at the entrance to Coos Bay, found the steamer for Marshfield waiting; at which place I arrived in the afternoon of the same day. After a few days spent in Marshfield, I went to Sumner, which is twelve miles distant, and reached by a small yacht, which had to be propelled with oars the greater part of the way on account of lack of sufficient wind in the slough through which we journeyed.

Returning to Marshfield, I prepared for a trip to points on the Coquille River—the "Sunny Coquille," of which a few writers have made mention and which empties into the ocean at Bandon, some distance south of Empire City. Mr. W. S. Vanderberg, of Marshfield, in giving me information regarding the route had mentioned that a part of the journey had to be made by rail, but that the cars were "not Pullmans;" yet I took the steamer by which I was to reach the railroad, in serene ignorance of what was before me. The steamer's course was up one of the numerous sloughs reaching out from Coos Bay, and just as we arrived in sight of the wharf at which we were to land, we ran aground. Seeing by the soundings that we were on the very edge of the channel, I remarked somewhat impatiently that if the men were like those in any other place, they would shove the boat off, not noticing to whom I had spoken.

"They ver-ry lekly know their bus'ness," said a peculiarly disagreeable voice.

Turning, I saw an Englishman of the nondescript class that is a disgrace to its country, and answering that possibly they did, but it had been my experience that they generally did not, I paid no more attention to him.

After waiting two hours for the tide, though within twenty-five feet of the shore, we reached the wharf and found the "train" waiting for us.

A diminutive engine, so unlike a railroad engine in form that no one would have suspected its pretensions in that direction, was standing on a track about three feet wide, and attached to it was a van, open on each side in the center and so swayed over as to suggest its having been resurrected from a recent wreck. The entrance to the van was at the end, and a seat ran along each side of the latter half of the inclosed part. In this we took seats, and when the "train" was ready to start, there were two quarters of beef, a carcass of a sheep, several oil cans, a dog, five women and nine men, not including the engineer, on board. Added to this happy combination was the fact that, there being no turn-table, the engine could not be placed at the front of the van, and we were to be backed over to the other end of the road. The track ran over high and crumbling trestles in places, and as it was extremely rough, the swaying of the van was frightful. Everybody was more or less alarmed, but the Englishman was the picture of abject fear.

As he clung to the side of the van too frightened to sit down, he looked towards me and began: "I've traveled many miles—but I never saw—such management as this—"

"Oh," I remarked, "they very likely know their business," and my revenge was complete.

We finally stopped where a trestle had been washed out by high water and were told that there was a mile of the car route that must be made by wagons. But where were the wagons? A one-seated vehicle stood before us, and fourteen pairs of eyes were turned on it in questioning dismay. As usual, the men all walked, but as one seat would hardly accommodate five women, the men in charge concluded to put another seat in the wagon, and after much deliberation, succeeded in bringing one out of its muddy seclusion only to find it so badly out of repair as to be useless.

After expectorating tobacco juice over several feet of territory, one of the men suddenly remarked, "We might hitch to the sleigh."

A rude sleigh lay half buried in the mud a few feet from where we stood, and as the men were binding the whiffletrees on with ropes, in the absence of the proper irons, I asked one of the women present if sufficient snow fell in that section to warrant the use of sleighs.

"Why, that's an Oregon buggy," she answered, and explained that such vehicles were made with a view to traveling over mud quite as much as snow.

Not aspiring to anything higher under the circumstances, I took a seat in the sleigh, and we were dragged over the distance at a sacrifice of horse flesh that would soon overbalance the gain of such methods. The rest of the trip to the Coquille River, a distance of six miles, was made in a large row-boat down a tortuous passage called Beaver Slough. In many places the bends were so abrupt and frequent that it was necessary for the passengers to assist in guiding the boat by grasping the overhanging bushes and swinging its prow into the channel, and the slough was at many points too narrow for the sweep of the oars. When within a mile of the Coquille, the oarsmen began to feel the effect of the incoming tide, and taking a long rope from the boat, went ashore and towed our bark the remaining distance to the river, where we waited an hour on a floating wharf for the steamer that was to take us to Coquille City, which is about midway between Bandon and Central Point; the latter being at the head of navigation for steamers.

Lest the reader should imagine that the route just described passes through a region but recently penetrated by settlers, and necessarily lacking in the facilities of modern travel, I will add that young men and women born and raised near it, cannot remember when the unique railroad was built, and an old gentleman whom I asked how long passengers had been brought through Beaver Slough, answered, "Well on to forty years."

Coquille City is on the right bank of the river as one faces the ocean, and stands upon a fairly even surface just above high water mark. Having a southern aspect and being far enough from the mouth of the river to escape the ocean winds, it is very inviting in appearance, and, as a railroad was in process of construction from Marshfield to the town, numerous improvements were being made. Like nearly all of the river and bay towns, its principal industry is in lumber, as timber of many beautiful and useful kinds grows in that section.

Myrtle Point, about twenty miles from Coquille, is similarly situated, but is nearer the abrupt rise of the coast range of hills. The valley has long been settled, and farms on the river range in value from forty to one hundred dollars an acre. Bandon gets the full force of the ocean breezes, but is a lovely summer resort, having a long line of picturesque beach to the southward and many points from which grand ocean views may be had.

Returning to Marshfield by the same route over which I had gone, the experience was even more eventful than before. The row-boat being so heavily laden that the oarsmen became exhausted, the passengers were obliged to "take a hand," and the ludicrous picture of a slight built young Hebrew commercial traveler, as he stood up in the boat, clad in a storm-coat reaching to his shoe soles and waving a dripping oar from one side to the other in his good-natured but *outre* attempts to assist, comes to me with convulsing force as I write. On reaching the steamer's wharf, at the end of the non-descript railroad, we found the tide out and the steamer fast aground, as usual. Seven hours to wait, with empty stomachs and no shelter but a fireless wharf house, was the prospect before us; but by walking half a mile or more we reached a camp of men engaged in building the new Coos Bay R. R., where we were given such food as the men had to offer, and a well warmed tent to sit in till midnight, at which time we reached the steamer by small boats. On the return journey from Scottsburg to Drain, I found the mountain shrubs clothed in a wealth of bloom so charming as to divert the thoughts from all hardships and cause the memory of the route to remain in the mind as a beautiful picture, instead of a valley of sighs.

Going to Portland and remaining through the State W. C. T. U. Convention and Pacific Coast Conference, I then returned to Southern Oregon, visiting Riddle's, Glendale, Grant's Pass, Medford, Jacksonville, Talent and Ashland, the last being but a short distance from the California line. Ashland is the largest town in the famed fruit section of Southern Oregon, and depends mainly upon that industry for its support, although the surrounding country is full of mines of greater or less value. Fruit grows without irrigating as a general thing, and the amount produced from the space devoted to the purpose is a source of much astonishment to those unacquainted with the country.

Mrs. Annie H. H. Russell, whose guest I was during a part of my stay in Ashland, is one of the most remarkable women I met with in my wanderings, and deserves a passing notice. Having been obliged to assist her husband, who is a marble cutter, in providing for the wants of a fast increasing family, Mrs. Russell began by designing embellishments for tombstones, and soon picking up the chisel and mallet, finally became so expert in their use that she far outstripped her husband, and now leads where she once followed. From poverty, they have reached affluence, and yet Mrs. Russell is the mother of eleven children and has found time to lead the W. C. T. U. forces for years. To her I was indebted for a drive among the foothills of the Siskyeu Mountains, where she pointed out many places of interest, among them being an immense granite block deposited on the top of a high peak by some unimaginable force and called Pilot Rock; which landmark has restored to his bearings many a footsore "forty-niner" and other bewildered traveler on the old "overland trail," not far from where we viewed it.

Returning northward again, I finally visited Hillsboro, Forest Grove and many other towns on the west side of the Willamette River, where I witnessed the process of harvesting in the large wheat fields.

"You must see a cook-wagon," said Mrs. S. A. McKune, whose guest I was at Amity, a small station on the railroad running from Portland to Corvallis.

Accordingly, we drove out to an immense field and viewed the harvesting outfit, which consisted of a reaper, a thresher—both run by steam —and a large covered wagon having a cooking range in the front end and narrow tables running along each side. The wagon was open at the sides, and on the outside were hinged seats, which could be let down when not in use. A bright young lady school teacher was "head cook," and, with two assistants, seemed to be spending her vacation quite as satisfactorily to herself as though wading the surf on the coast with her comrades. A diminutive tent stood at a little distance from the wagon, and the young lady told me that she and her assistants lodged there, while the men carried blankets and slept in the straw piles.

"We are protected from rudeness or insult, and are paid the same wages as the men, or we would not remain," she assured me; and as I thought of the pale shop girls in the cities, breathing vile air and working for half pay, the situation; with open air exercise and good wages, seemed Paradisical by contrast.

CHAPTER XI.

On the morning of September 14, 1891, I started eastward from Portland by way of the Union Pacific R. R., and knowing that the country to Hood River, a distance of sixty miles, was as yet unbroken by the W. C. T. U. plowshare, I determined to make a thorough exploration of the route, which determination gave me a view of two of the most beautiful sights witnessed on the Pacific Slope. Stopping at a small place called Fairview, I formed a society and inquired what was beyond.

"Latourelle Falls is the next place of any size," said the pastor of whom I made the inquiry.

Not finding the place on my guide book, I was somewhat perplexed, but being assured that the town was one of the older ones on the Columbia, which the Union Pacific R. R. follows for a good distance from Portland, I concluded to visit it and see for myself. Consequently, I was landed on an unsheltered platform on the bank of the Columbia a short time after leaving Fairview, and soon found my way to the residence of the superintendent of a large lumber mill, which seemed to be the one place of activity in the town. And then the secret of the town's obscurity came to light. The story was that a Mr. Latourelle had journeyed up the Columbia and pitched his tent at that point long before the river's mighty cliffs had echoed to the sound of a railroad whistle, and that as the years passed, finding solitude was still solitude, however beautiful, he had taken to himself an Indian woman as wife. Finally paleface civilization came along and brought with it a railroad, which Mr. Latourelle quite naturally welcomed, but which Mrs. Latourelle, quite as naturally, could not see the need of. The former affixed his signature to the document giving the railroad company the right of way through the Latourelle estate, but his native companion flatly refused to aid or abet any such enterprise. As a consequence, the document lacked a name, and until that should be supplied, the railroad company purposed ignoring the existence of the town as far as practicable, and would neither build a depot, allow the name of the station on their guide books nor even check baggage to the place. It was a contest of wills between the Indian woman and the great U. P. R. R. Co , but the lastest accounts showed the former to be pursuing the even tenor of her way in un moved contempt of the powerful corporation.

But, those who visit Latourelle Falls will not wonder that the Indians, the first possessors, are attached to the place. Just back of the town and but a short walk from it, is a waterfall so unlike any of the many others to be seen, and surrounded by such wild and unusual scenery as to cause one to wonder why so little is known of it by the public. A road ending in a narrow path along the base of a high wall of rock leads to the fall, and as my companion led the way around an angle in the wall, I found, facing me, a beetling cliff over which a body of water was falling, clear of all obstructions, a distance of, probably, two hundred feet, and striking in a pool of mysterious depth below. As no measurement had been made by any with whom I talked, I could not learn the exact depth of the fall, but give the distance mentioned as an estimate. Quite in keeping with the surroundings, we felt a tremor of the earth under our feet as we stood gazing at the fall, and afterwards found that it was the advance agent of a sharper earthquake shock later in the evening.

Many have heard of Bridal Veil Falls, and have seen the picture of a stream flowing over a contracted space on a mountain's side and widening out like a veil as it descends, but there are, doubtless, some in whose minds the picture is associated, as it was in the writer's, with ungraspable solitudes of nature, and to such, a brief description of actual experience may not be uninteresting. Having been given the name of the treasurer of the Bridal Veil Lumbering Co. by the superintendent at Latourelle, through whose interest and that of his family I met with a fair measure of success at the latter place, on arriving at Bridal Veil station, I inquired for the treasurer and was agreeably surprised to find the gentleman to be Mr. J. S. Bradly, formerly of Newark, Ohio.

"We live rather high, out here," jocosely remarked Mr. Bradly, pointing to a beautiful cottage on an immense bluff of the Columbia, as he led the way to his residence; "but" he added, "I think you will like the view when you once get up."

The house is reached by a stairway similar to those in the Sound country, but constructed with more of a view to ease of ascent, and having seats for rest and observation. The top of the eminence is level for a considerable space, giving ample room for the cottage and its grounds, and commands a view of the Columbia both up and down the stream; while to the right of the cottage runs a deep gorge, down which a lumber flume is built from the mills above, and across which is a high mountain with a wagon road cut into its side far above the peak of the cottage tower.

The company's plant extends from the station

of Bridal Veil, where a large supply store is located and where the lumber is taken from the flume for shipment, two miles up into the hills, and five miles inland in the deep forest of the highlands, making seven miles in all. At the end of the two first miles is Glenwood, where the mills are located, and where the president of the company, Mr. L. C. Palmer, resides. Appointments were made at both places, and after speaking at the station, I prepared to try the mountain road. A trip from the station to the mills is usually made three times a week in good weather by a wagon carrying supplies, and in that conveyance, which was drawn by five mules, one of which was ridden by the driver, I took a seat in the early morning of a bright autumn day, amidst numerous sacks and packages as firmly lashed on as for a storm at sea. As we began the steep ascent, I soon found that such an occurrence as being unseated and dashed over a precipice was quite possible, and firmly grasping a cross rope of the lashings with one hand, and slipping the fingers of the other through a large link pendent from a chain with which the forward part of the wagon was bound, I prepared for emergencies. The driver was often obliged to stop and give his heated team a breathing spell, at which times I could relax my vigilance and enjoy the wonderful view across the deep canyon. In places, the sight of the abrupt descent but a foot or two from the track was more than even well trained nerves could bear, and in those spots, I literally "turned my face to the wall;" for the mountain side is nearly an upright wall the entire distance. And in that way I ascended from the valley below, to the heights above Bridal Veil Falls.

From Glenwood, a well built railroad owned by the company runs the remaining five miles, being the means by which the supply of timber is brought to the mills, and arrangements had been made that I should be taken over the road, that I might miss no opportunity of sight-seeing. Accordingly, soon after luncheon, which was in preparation when we reached Glenwood, I accompanied Mr. and Mrs. Palmer in the wildest of wild rides in an engine cab for half the length of the road, and on a log car the remaining distance, to vary the experience.

"There are several stations on the way," shouted Mr. Palmer, as he clung by an iron rail to the outside of the bounding, swaying cab, "but you may miss them if you don't keep a sharp lookout."

The "stations" referred to were occasional cabins occupied by claim holders, who seemed to enjoy our novel "excursion" quite as much as we. On we went, over trestles and around curves, sometimes in deep woods, and sometimes passing large tracts of fallen timber, till we reached the terminus, where a few deserted cabins stood, which Mr. Palmer humorously assured me constituted a town, bearing the mysterious name of "Goblin"; having been christened in honor of an apparition that was said to roam in the vicinity.

The waterfall has been too often pictured by travelers to need any mention here, and is faithfully portrayed in the illustrated guides; but a feat accomplished by Mrs. Bradley and a friend has not been chronicled.

"I once walked that two miles to the mills on a plank a foot wide," said Mrs. Bradley, as we sat before the fire after my return from Glenwood.

"How?" I asked, in great surprise.

"You may well ask, but I cannot myself tell how I did it. Yet, I did accomplish the undertaking, and I have not yet recovered from the effects," she answered, and then continued: "You know the flume is built along the side of the canyon. Well, on a level with the bottom of the flume and resting on the same supports that hold it are planks a foot wide running the entire length of the flume, as a means by which it may be reached to make repairs. A young lady from Portland was visiting me, and being ready for adventure, insisted on attempting the feat of walking up to the mills. I at last consented to accompany her, and we started. There was no lumber being sent down the flume at the time, but when we had proceeded so far that turning back was impossible—for we soon learned that going up was much easier than coming down—the men, not knowing, of course, that we were on the way, began sending down railroad timber, and as every little obstruction of the current of water caused spray to dash over the side of the flume upon us, every thread in our garments was soon drenched. My young son was with us, but he was as helpless as we. To have turned back, would have been certain death, and our only hope was in going forward and endeavoring to avoid the force of the spray, which, if we had received it in full, would have knocked us off the plank. Lumber, too, often shoots over the sides of the flume, and you can imagine where we would have been if any had struck us. The distance to the rocks below us was eighty feet at one place, and, to add to our horror, when we reached it we found the planks on which we walked were so far below the flume, to which we had held as we went along, that we could barely touch it with our finger tips.

"Yet, you went on to the mills without accident!" I exclaimed, not thinking such a feat possible!"

"Yes—that is, I did," she answered. "My young friend climbed upon the bank just before we reached the mills, but I went on to the end. I did not realize how much my nervous system had suffered until afterwards : but the picture of that awful chasm still comes before my eyes at night, sometimes, and I cannot rest."

And those who gaze down the canyon at Bridal Veil will not wonder that nerves were overtaxed by such an experience.

In contrast to a great number of similar companies found in the West, the Bridal Veil Lumbering Co. closes its supply store on Sunday, forbids the use of liquor on its grounds, and has established week day and Sunday schools for the education of the children of its employes. The result is that the four hundred men employed make up, with their families, an intelligent, well-dressed body, which would be a credit to any community.

Proceeding to Cascade Locks, where the great locks of the Columbia were in process of construction by the United States Government, I found a town said to contain five hundred people, but without either church building or service, although possessing nine flourishing saloons. Upon inquiring where public meetings were held, I was informed that, a part of the inhabitants being Roman Catholic, and a part Protestant, creeds had so warred against piety that no meetings of any kind were allowed in the schoolhouse, the only public building in the place. The outlook seemed forbidding, but so easy of access is humanity's better side that the use of the hall owned by the M. W. of A., the only one in the town, was given me gratuitously and was well filled.

Rain was falling when I left Cascade Locks, which was on September 22nd, but on arriving at Hood River I began to realize that I was again entering the arid region. The familiar dust was everywhere, but as Dr. Thomas, whose wife, Mrs. L. R. Thomas, was superintendent of the department of Juvenile Work of the Oregon W. C. T. U., met me at the station, I lost sight of the unpleasant features in the realization that I was to enjoy a rest from pioneering.

Mount Hood, which has become a resort for summer tourists, is reached from Hood River station by wagon road, but my time would not admit of more than a drive in its direction far enough to get a breath of the air chilled by its mighty glacier. Fruit grows well in the vicinity, and those who are wise enough to engage in its culture will reap a harvest of dollars from future pilgrims to the wonderful mountain, which is said to still send up occasional puffs of vapor from its heated depths.

Having passed three very pleasant days at Hood River, I took the train for The Dalles, which is a town of over two thousand inhabitants, but had recently been visited by a destructive fire.

There Mrs. Lee, wife of Hon. J. D. Lee, met me and showed me the devastated territory where a thriving little city had stood but a short time before.

"What was the cause of the fire?" I asked.

"Whisky," was the answer; and in that one word was summed up the cause of the loss of hundreds of thousands of dollars in business blocks; the destruction of churches, city buildings and homes; and of hundreds of people being without food or clothing.

But the United States Government, and the great state of Oregon had received their revenue!

The W. C. T. U. Reading-room had escaped destruction, and the members of the society had risen rapidly in the estimation of the sufferers, many of whom had invited the town's destruction by licensing the liquor traffic.

The name was given to the place, by French explorers, from the fact that at that point the Columbia is broken by rocky barriers, producing numerous falls and rapids. The Dalles is at the beginning of the arid country, and the river above that point is spoken of as the upper Columbia, while below, it is designated as the lower Columbia.

Finding the name "Grant's" coming next on the list of places marked as needing my attention,

I accordingly embarked for that place; being blissfully ignorant of the predominance, in some places, and persistent aggressiveness of Columbia River sand. Arriving at Grant's, I found a small cluster of buildings on a stretch of sand that would have been level had it not been drifted into windrows, and that varied the monotony of lying inert by rising up in generous sections on the wings of a strong breeze that was blowing, and striking one's flesh with the sting of insects. My first inquiry was when the next train would pass, but as the baggagemen, true to the reputation of their class, had crushed my traveling trunk—which, by the way, was both small and strong, offering no temptation to over-strained muscles—I was obliged to see what I thought to be my only hope pass, in the form of a local freight train, before my baggage could be put in traveling condition. Finding that the place did not possess an audience room of any description, I gazed out over the desolate waste of sand in a vain attempt to determine what to do next, while the agent tried to excuse the ruining of the trunk, and a man whose breath smelled of liquor assured me he was a "temperance man," and had been "one of them when they were running," but that they had "all gone away now"—which last I was quite ready to believe. And then, dear sisters of the W. C. T. U., and those, too, who do not know the magic of our badge, just then I caught the gleam of a white ribbon under a wind blown dust wrap, worn by a small woman who seemed to have drifted in on a sand cloud.

On my explaining the situation, the lady, (whose name I have lost and vainly written for) said, "I live across the river, at Columbus, three miles from here, and you must go home with me;" then explaining that she was secretary of the Columbus, Wash., W. C. T. U.

"But, how do you get there?" I asked; as the Columbia is both wide and swift at that point.

"Oh, I have a boat," she said, "and if the river is too rough for that, there is a ferry a half mile below."

Having my baggage stored, we went to the river, and finding the waves too high for safety, walked the half mile to the ferry in sand shoe deep and crossed over to the Washington shore.

Columbus is one of the older towns on the upper Columbia and lies on an interval between the water's edge and the high bluff which was, doubtless, once the bank of the river, and which at that point makes a sharp curve, thus sheltering the town from the sandstorms brought by the up stream gales. The place is a shipping point for great quantities of fine fruit, which is raised in orchards adjacent to the town, and I there for the first time saw peaches and grapes growing to perfection in Washington. My host and hostess, Mr. and Mrs. Hicenbothem, had settled in the place twenty-five years before, when Indians were their principal associates, and they both laughed heartily at my experience.

"You have had a fine time compared with that of the first women who came here in the interest of the Union," said Mr. H. "Did you ever hear how Mrs. Reese crossed the river from here?"

Having read an official report of the pioneer organizer Mrs. Mary Bynon Reese, in which she mentioned a perilous trip across the Columbia in a row-boat, I answered that I had read of it.

"But you probably did not get the whole of it. I do not think Mrs. Reese ever knew all the facts," said he, and then proceeded to tell the story: "The way it was, Mrs. Reese had to be taken over to the railroad before daylight, to reach the train, and I concluded to take her to Biggs station, as that is nearer than Grant's, and being down stream, we would not have to pull against the current. There are rapids close to the station at Biggs, but the passage is safe enough in daylight, and I did not anticipate any trouble; although the Columbia is a treacherous stream at best. So I took an Indian with me to help row, and we started. But we had not gone far before

I found that the current shifted the boat around in an unusual way, and as we could not see where we were, I began to feel uneasy. Yet, I did not think there was any danger, and as we had to pull with all our might, there was not much time to listen for the sound of the rapids. Mrs. Reese did not seem to be much frightened, and I was afraid to say anything for fear of making matters worse. But all at once I heard a rush of water over the rocks and knew we were in for it. Mrs. Reese said it was 'awful rough,' but I nudged the Indian, and he never opened his mouth. I expected an upset, which would, probably, have been death for all of us, but I hoped for the best, and in less time than I can tell it, we were in smooth water and close to a place where we could land. We did not tell Mrs. Reese, and I do not believe she knows to this day that she actually went over the rapids."

As I crossed the river on my return to Grant's three days later, I was given some information that seemed to throw light on the mysterious fluctuation of the current of which Mr. Hicenbothem had spoken, but which information was not of a nature to inspire one with a feeling of personal safety or an inclination to search further into the mystery. A young man in charge of the matters of a company that had undertaken the construction of a portage railroad on the Washington shore kindly volunteered to row over to Grant's with me, thus saving me the long walk in the sand from the ferry, and as we coasted up the shore to a favorable point for crossing, he told me of the character of the bottom of the stream as shown by soundings.

"There will be twenty feet of water in one place, and not more than one in another not six feet away," said he. Pointing towards a perfectly bare and perpendicular cliff that rose out of the water a short distance before us, he asked: "Do you see how smooth the water is at the base of that cliff?"

Noticing that the water for a considerable space seemed entirely undisturbed, I answered in the affirmative, and he continued: "When we were surveying along here, we undertook to sound that place, and as no line seemed to reach the bottom, we thought there must be a current that swept it along, and so we tried sinking a hundred foot cable with a big buoy attached; but, cable, buoy and all went out of sight, and we have never been able to find them."

Our boat was entering on the still water as he ceased speaking, and the horror of the unfathomed depth beneath me overcame all desire to know more. Yet, it would seem probable that a sink of such dimensions would receive an influx from subterranean sources, at times, that would interfere with its serenity and cause fluctuations at its surface.

Proceeding to Arlington, which is also on the river, I found a small town over which the sand was drifting at a rate that promised entire obliteration. A number of stage lines running into the interior center of that point, producing some activity in business, yet, no attempt had been made to build wind breaks to protect the place, and many of the shops were deserted, which added to the general appearance of desolation. While there, I learned, both by observation and experience, the meaning of the term, "sand-lapping," which I had heard used once or twice by countrymen. The sand is driven into the pores with such force by the strong winds that the lips become rough, and lapping them into flexibility with the tongue is instinctively resorted to. Hence, "Sand-lappers of the Upper Columbia" is a title that should take its place beside "Sound Clam-diggers" and "Willamette Web-feet."

Pendleton, eighty-eight miles east of Arlington and over eight hundred feet farther skyward, is the largest town in Eastern Oregon, and is situated in the productive valley of the Umatilla River. Several Indian women in bright colored satin dresses presented a novel sight as I walked to the residence of Mrs. N. E. De Spain, on my arrival, and I learned they were from the Umatilla reservation, near the town. Mission schools had been established among the Umatillas many years before, and the result was an industrious and prosperous tribe. Pendleton is noted for nothing else as much, perhaps, as its intelligent inhabitants. Being settled from the better classes of Eastern and Southern people, it has less of the sensational in its makeup than many other towns, and consequently has the appearance of being older. It has a population of nearly five thousand, and has schools, churches and business places equal to those in even larger towns. The Union Pacific has a branch from there to Spokane Falls, and a branch of the Northern Pacific reaches there from Pasco.

From Pendleton, a jaunt of thirty-six miles on the Spokane branch of the Union Pacific brought me to Athena, Weston and Milton, the latter being near the Oregon line and but a short distance from Walla Walla, in Washington. The country was extremely dry, yet I saw fine fruit in abundance, and large patches of delicious melons lay rotting in the dust for want of purchasers.

Returning to Pendleton, I continued on the main line to La Grande, seventy-five miles distant, the first fifty miles of which make a rise of over three thousand feet to Kamela, where the altitude is over four thousand feet above sea level, being the highest reached by the Union Pacific in Oregon. I found La Grande in a high state of excitement over a recent murder and the probable solution of the mystery surrounding two committed a short time before. The body of one of the murdered men had been sent on to Portland in an empty car, and that of another discovered under a pile of coal, but the third had been found in a saloon ; his murderers either lacking opportunity or becoming too intoxicated, as was supposed, to dispose of it. The proprietor and employes of the saloon had been arrested, and the pitiful yet disgusting spectacle of men who had given their influence towards the perpetuation of such crimes by licensing the sale of liquor, clamoring for the strangling of those who had been maddened to murder by its use, was again before the public.

At Elgin, twenty-one miles up a branch of the Union Pacific, I found the women arrayed as in Gardiner, for the defense of their homes, while the men, with some exceptions, were inviting ruin by favoring the erection of a brewery. Union, my next stopping point on the main line, is the county seat of Union county, in which La Grande and Elgin are located, and I there visited the county buildings. As I went into the jail, I saw an iron cage eight or ten feet square, in which eight souls, men and boys, were huddled promiscuously, and on inquiring, I found that three were supposed to be murderers—not yet having been tried—and the remaining five were accused of comparatively trivial offenses. The faces of several showed a pallor that was shocking, and I asked how long they had been confined in such close quarters.

"I have been in this cage thirteen months," said one.

"You are allowed to come out every day for exercise, I suppose," I said.

"I have been out just four times since I have been here," he answered.

And I found his answer to be correct. Some prisoners had escaped many months before, and the sheriff remarked in explanation of the state of affairs, that he did not "mean to be blamed again." So, most shocking cruelty was being deliberately practiced that justice (?) might not be thwarted!

In answer to my question as to how many came to imprisonment through the use of intoxicating liquor, five promptly admitted its direct agency, and in five other cases it was found to have been the indirect cause; which left but one of the total eleven in the jail untouched by its blight. Not so much as a line of reading matter had been furnished the men, yet the town had several churches, and two expounders of the Scriptures were playing croquet but a short distance from the jail.

Visits to North Powder, Baker City and Huntington completed the Oregon work, and Idaho was before me.

CHAPTER XII.

Sage, rock and dust, varied by sparse patches of timber with "magnificent distances" between, and occasional glimpses of the Snake River and its diminutive tributaries make up the scenery in Southern Idaho along the line of the Union Pacific R. R.

Weiser, Payette and Caldwell are the principal towns between the Oregon line and Nampa, from which place a branch runs to Boise City, the state capital. Caldwell is distinguished from the other towns by a foundation of alkali so pure that to indulge in a flower or vegetable garden, it is necessary to have several inches of the surface scraped away and replaced by productive earth.

At Nampa I reached the home of Mrs. Sarah H. Black, president of the Idaho W. C. T. U., whose husband, Rev. James P. Black, is pastor of the Presbyterian Church at that place. From Nampa I went to Boise City, where I remained three days. The country from Nampa to Boise City is level valley land, and very productive with irrigation. I saw several large orchards of young trees, and was told that fruit growing was likely to become one of the principal industries. Very few evidences of wheat raising were visible, but close cropped alfalfa made a green carpet over all the fields where the sage brush had been cleared away. Machines for pulling sage brush were in operation within sight from the car windows, and the uprooted bushes were to be seen piled in large heaps near the houses, for fuel. Boise City has the pleasant feature of plenty of shade trees, being easily irrigated from the adjacent hills, and bears indications of having been a thriving town before a railroad reached it. I there met Mrs. J. C. Straughan, who was appointed one of the commissioners to the Columbian Exposition from Idaho, and found in her one of the principal W. C. T. U. workers of the state.

At Mountain Home, a small town fifty-five miles east of Nampa and about four hundred feet above that place, the wild rabbits hopped familiarly out of the sage to greet me as I walked through the town, and seemed to be all the inhabitants at home except the saloon keepers. The only church building in the place was controlled by the Episcopalians, who would neither hold services in it themselves, nor allow any other denomination to do so, and I learned that a Presbyterian missionary had but a few days before been refused the use of the schoolhouse for a meeting, although there had been no religious services in the town, which had recently become a county seat, for a year. Yet, Idaho had disfranchised the Mormons, ostensibly on account of their religious belief.

Proceeding to the Court House, I made some remarks on consistency that soon secured me an audience room ; but a doubt still lingers in my mind as to whether the first inhabitants, the companionable rabbits, have been greatly improved upon in that little hamlet, the principal street of which is an almost unbroken line of saloons. There were some shining exceptions to the general apathetic obtuseness, among them being the probate judge, the deputy sheriff's family and a few others, but they made up so small a minority that improvement seemed yet far away.

At Glenn's Ferry, I found a reading-room, supported by the U. P. R. R. Co. and conducted by the Y. M. C. A. ; which is but one of a number established in the same way along the line of the road, as safeguards against demoralization from the hardships and loneliness incident to railroad life in a new country. By much effort the secretary in charge had succeeded in having services held in the schoolhouse, the only public building, every Sabbath, which drew many men from the saloons.

Shoshone is a town of perhaps one thousand

inhabitants, and has one church building and a resident pastor (Methodist). The W. C. T. U. has there a free reading-room and has done much towards building up the town. Mrs. A. S. Senter, president of the local Union, is one of Idaho's intelligent and clear-sighted women, and, with her able assistants, wields an influence much needed in that infant state.

The presence of snow, and an increasing chilliness in the atmosphere admonished me not to risk a snow blockade by attempting a trip on the Wood River branch from Shoshone to Ketchum, and I continued on a hundred miles to Pocatello, from which point the Ogden, Butte and Helena branch runs northward to Helena, Mont., by which route Yellowstone Park is reached, and southward to Ogden and Salt Lake City.

At Pocatello, Mrs. H. V. Platt kindly invited me to a drive over the town, and I witnessed the singular sight of a city on wheels. The buildings, which were mostly cottages, had been built on railroad land with the privilege of removal at such time as an Indian reservation adjoining should be opened to purchasers, and that time having arrived, the town had taken up its bed, board and habitation and was in process of migration to a foundation of its own. Gold had been discovered close to the city, and high hopes of a "boom" were being entertained.

A trip to Yellowstone Park in December was not desirable, and as the delay caused by visits to the towns on the branch towards Helena might throw me into snow drifts in Wyoming, I concluded to turn southward from Pocatello, and finding Oxford to be first on my list, I took a train about four o'clock of a chilly morning for that place. Having made careful inquiry as to whether Oxford was immediately on the railroad, or some distance away, and been assured that the track ran through the town, I was somewhat surprised when, an hour after leaving Pocatello, I was set down on the platform of a lone station out of sight of any other building.

"Where is the town?" I asked.

"Two miles from here," the agent answered.

And as I looked around for some conveyance, he said there was no regular hack running from the station, but that he carried the mail into the town on a pony and would send a conveyance for me.

"You will have to lock yourself in while I am gone," said he, "for there are tramps around here sometimes;" and with that precautionary information, he mounted his pony and rode away, leaving me in sole possession.

An hour afterwards a conveyance arrived, but a snow storm had come on in the meantime, and on reaching the only hotel in the place, I found it kept by a Mormon bishop, all the members of whose family, including himself, had but just returned from a dancing party and had retired precipitantly, not concerning themselves about possible guests sufficiently to build a fire. They were finally aroused, and after breakfast, I found the Methodist pastor, to whom I had been directed.

It was thought best for me to remain over Sunday, and as I had never heard a Mormon preacher on his "native heath," I attended the Mormon service, which was in the afternoon, in company with the Methodist pastor.

Arriving at the church, which was heated—or, rather, was not heated—by a small wood-burning stove, we found perhaps forty chilled looking persons assembled, and very soon a half-dozen roughly dressed men filed in, and proceeding to a platform running across the end of the church, took their seats in a row on a bench placed there for the purpose.

The bishop had recovered from his Terpsichorean dissipation, and opened the meeting by saying that the sacrament would then be partaken of, and requesting the choir to sing. As soon as the singing began, a boy clad in blue overalls grasped a zinc bucket which stood on the platform, or pulpit, and passed through the congregation to the door. He soon returned, and, placing the bucket, now full of water, on the platform, proceeded to hunt up and rinse out a couple of goblets, which he filled by plunging them into the bucket and spilling the water over the platform;—all quite in keeping with the dismal surroundings, of sleet outside and the shivering audience within. An old gentleman then took a plate of bread and passed through the congregation, the boy following with the water.

At the completion of the observance of that form, the bishop introduced a Mr. Kimball as the speaker to whom we were to listen, and the gentleman arose. He began by saying that knowledge always had been and always would be revealed to those receiving it, and that in no other way than by revelation could any knowledge of spiritual matters be acquired. He then cited the prophets and spoke of the possibility of "talking with God" as well in modern as in ancient times, and seemed in a fair way to soon arrive at the "revelations" of Joseph Smith, when his memory evidently failed him, and he rambled in a vain search for a revelation that would bring him back to his subject.

Yet, he talked on. The fire went out and the children cried, but still he talked; and we were obliged to take our departure before he closed his remarks.

Logan, one of the oldest towns in Utah, was

my first stopping place in that territory, and the picture it presented in the blue-gold light of the Indian summer-like day on which I arrived was charming enough to suggest the exclamation, "If this be a product of Mormonism, farewell Gentiles!"

Wide streets, beautiful and substantial buildings in a wilderness of shade trees, and the white turrets of a Mormon temple standing out in bold relief from a background of deep blue haze which but partially obscured the outlines of a fir-clad mountain-side constituted the view that met the gaze from a distance, and a nearer approach showed well stocked stores and shops teeming with customers, and a remarkable absence of saloons and drunkenness.

Missions, established by both the Methodists and Presbyterians, have long existed at Logan, and have, without doubt, had their influence against Mormonism; but the town itself, aside from the two Gentile churches and school buildings, is the product of Mormon thrift, and the municipal government is controlled by Mormon votes. No squalor is anywhere visible, although the population is about five thousand, and I was told that cases of want were very rare.

"But, what of the women—are they not dreadfully treated?" some one will ask.

And I answer, "No."

The burden of hardship was lifted from the Mormon women by the abolition of polygamy, and their condition is now no more to be lamented over than that of women in general. The United States Government made provision for the care of such of the polygamous wives as should become homeless by the abolishment of polygamy, but comparatively few have had to avail themselves of the Government's bounty; and the Mormon women are today the more zealous defenders of their faith.

"But, do these facts show merit in Mormonism?" will be the question asked after reading this apparent eulogy.

So far as Mormonism is considered as a religion—a means for the development of the spiritual nature, the answer must invariably be "No:" but as a patriarchal form of government, it has the merit of having taught its people industry, economy, peaceableness and a partial self-denial and temperance. Its fatal fault is that it has cultivated these virtues to a temporal, instead of a spiritual, end. Even the little spirituality Mormonism professes is so tinted with carnality that it appears only in a debased form, and is not worthy of consideration.

But the debasing days are over, and the Latter Day Saints will soon be spoken of in the past tense. The institution of Mormonism was, practically, founded on and held together by polygamy, and robbed of that, nothing remains but a few forms and ceremonies, from which the people will soon fall away, being prompted to their observance by neither faith nor fear—the first never having existed, and the last being removed.

After a visit to Franklin, back across the line into Idaho, I proceeded to Ogden, making a short stop and continuing on to Salt Lake City, where I met the active W. C. T. U. workers of the Territory and held two public meetings. Being entertained in the hospitable home of Mrs. E. H. Parsons, whose husband, Hon. E. H. Parsons, is United States Marshal for Utah, my stay was a very enjoyable one, and I was given an opportunity to judge of the existing state of affairs by personal observation.

One of the first convictions that is forced upon the understanding of the observer is that, although possessing a good share of dissipation and many places for indulgence in intoxicants, Salt Lake City is yet not as bad in that respect as many places of its size in the West. The habit of temperance in the use of intoxicating liquors, so long cultivated by the Mormons, had not, I found, entirely lost its force; but the fact that it was fast becoming submerged by the incoming tide propelled by party politics was easy of discernment, and led to a mental query regarding the advisability of "jumping out of the frying-pan into the fire" by denouncing the Mormons and indorsing "Kate Field's party," as the Anti-Mormon party is often called in Utah.

Another thing that confronts the mental vision is the surprising picture of the devotees of Bacchus arrayed in defense of virtue! Among all the truly intelligent and Christian people with whom I had the opportunity of conversing, there was perfect unanimity in the opinion that, since polygamy had been abolished, there was no more to be feared from Mormonism than from several other isms extant, and it should be left to the usual evangelizing influences; but the friends of the wine cup say "No" to all such reasoning.

Politicians with faces flushed by intoxicating liquor, that great promoter of impurity, will sneer at temperance effort, and point with vehemence to Mormonism, with such remarks as, "There's where your work is needed! If Mormons get into the Government, we're gone!"

And these zealous patriots usually end with. "It takes a woman like Kate Field to do the right thing."

And then—well, one does not feel like envying Miss Field her associations.

But, all this affectation of zeal for the nation's welfare has a cause. Utah is aspiring to statehood, and the object of the politicians is to disfranchise the Mormons, as has been done in Idaho, that their opponents may gain a substantial and controlling foothold.

A W. C. T. U. restaurant occupying the lower floor of the headquarters of the Salt Lake City Union was in full operation, and efforts were being made by Mrs. Parsons, who led the enterprise, for its enlargement, that the needy might be reached by low prices. Public gospel meetings were held at the headquarters every Sunday evening, and the attendance on the one evening I was there was much larger than the seating capacity; which showed the interest that had been aroused. Miss Harriet E. Turner, president of the Union, had adopted the plan of standing at the entrance and inviting passers in; and many a mother's boy, alone and despondent in a strange land, has received a home-like welcome and been cheered by kind words at that open door.

In rambling over the city, I visited the Mormon Tabernacle, and obediently walked to the farther end while the gentleman in charge dropped a pin at the other, to demonstrate the wonderful acoustic properties of the audience room; but as I was not near enough to observe whether the good brother dropped a pin or a dollar, I can only say that my impression was that the meeting place of the Saints was more given to sound than show; no attempt at grandeur having been made in its construction.

CHAPTER XIII.

From Salt Lake City, I went to Evanston, Wyoming. remaining over one night and proceeding to Green River, in the same state. While there, where I remained four days, extremely cold weather came on, being the first I had experienced since leaving the East. Green River is among the older of Wyoming towns, but the aridity of the country is discouraging to enterprise, and the place is not prepossessing from any point of view.

Mrs. Dibble, president of the local society, and Mrs. R. A. Jones, secretary of the State Union, I found to be women of much intelligence, but having to work under many disadvantages, they had accomplished less than better circumstances would have assured.

At Rock Springs, fifteen miles east of Green River, are large coal mines, the discovery of which was the saving of that part of Wyoming from desertion by settlers, who, having used up the sparse timber supply, had no resource left for fuel.

Exorbitant prices are charged for the coal, which is of a good quality, the price per ton being from five to eight dollars while the cost at the mines is about seventy-five cents. The railroad company, doubtless, receives a large percentage of the profit, but that makes little difference to the unfortunate settler who is obliged to pay the bill.

As the train for Laramie, a long jaunt of two hundred and seventy miles, arrived at Rock Springs at a very early hour, I stepped into a car just at day-break only to find it crowded with sleepy passengers, with a few upright figures discernible in the dim light, but no vacant seats.

Immediately a young man arose and, coming forward, grasped my hand and, calling me by name, assured me his seat was at my service.

"I am one of those who signed the pledge at Salt Lake City, and I knew you as soon as you came in," he said.

He then sat down on the arm of the seat and told me something of his ramblings in the West in search of employment, sometimes successful and full of hope, but more often despondent over the prospect of becoming penniless from lack of work and high prices of living, and always missing the associations of his home, which he told me was in Canada.

"But I would get along all right if it were not for liquor. Somebody is always asking you to drink in this country, and before you know it, you have the habit," said he, and further remarked that he wished "the women could make the laws."

But I was to hear from the other side. Being sadly in need of sleep, I was roused from a partial doze some little time afterwards by the first words of the following dialogue :

Masculine voice—"We're in the state where the women vote."

Feminine voice—"What state is it?"

Masculine voice—"Wyoming! of course. Don't you know where the women vote?"

Feminine voice—"Do the women vote here? I think it's just horrid! Do you suppose they all do?"

At that point a second female voice broke in with the answer, "No, they don't all vote. I've lived here fourteen years, and I never voted yet."

First feminine voice—"I don't see how women find time to do men's work."

Second feminine voice—"Nor I either. I always find enough to do without having anything to do with politics."

After a few further remarks in the same vein, the conversation was dropped, but at the end of a few minutes the second feminine voice said: "John," (yes, dear reader, the name was really

John), "when we get to Rawlins, I want you to go to the store the first thing and get me Hilda; for if you don't you'll forget it."

"What?" in a new masculine voice.

"Hilda; H-i-l-d-a. It's a novel I hain't had."

"I thought you'd had about everything."

"Well, I have; but this is one I've just heard of, and they've got it up to Rawlins."

As I did not stop at Rawlins, which is a hundred miles or so from Rock Springs, I saw no more of the lady of non-political but literary tastes, but I afterwards learned that she was a fair specimen of the Wyoming women who do not exercise their rights as citizens.

The future of Wyoming will, I predict, be very different from its past. For many years the women labored under the disadvantage of being out-numbered by the male population, made up largely of foreigners, by about nineteen to one, as I was informed, and that circumstance, added to woman's unavoidable inexperience in governmental matters, and the hardships of pioneering in an extremely hard country, has retarded the bringing about of any great results; but equal suffrage has taken deep root, and now that the sun has risen on Wyoming, by her being granted statehood with an untrammeled population, the blossoming and fruit bearing seasons must soon follow.

That the leading men of the state are well satisfied with their female comrades in the field of politics, was shown by the remark of an old resident, a man of much influence in his part of the state.

"Why," said he, "we wouldn't have accepted statehood without the women. I don't know why it is," he continued, "but it has been my experience that a woman will vote right where a man won't dare to."

Laramie, which is next in size to Cheyenne, the largest city in the state, is an old town, and as it is situated in a fertile valley, has nothing of the dreariness of appearance possessed by many towns on the line of the Union Pacific R. R. To a traveler returning to the East, a slight touch of the feeling of home-coming is felt at Laramie, and the surroundings begin to take on a familiar appearance.

While there I conversed with several gentlemen regarding the matter of suffrage, and found the cry of the moral part of the male population to be, "Why do not the women help us?" which was perplexing as a question, but highly amusing as an evidence that woman was no longer looked upon as a "clinging vine," but as the helpmate God intended her to be.

"Why do you allow this cry to go out?" I

asked some of the ladies in the state, and the answer solved the mystery.

"We are not strong enough in number to nominate the candidates we would feel justified in voting for, and the best men we have do not always help *us*," one lady explained.

In speaking of a local election, another lady said, "There was not a man nominated that a respectable woman could vote for, and we could not get the best men we had to help us nominate the candidates we knew were honorable."

The highest altitude on the line of the Union Pacific R. R. is reached at Sherman, between Laramie and Cheyenne, the elevation being 8247 feet. A high cairn of rough stones stands, bare and uninclosed, on this height at the right of the track as one faces eastward, and on inquiry I was told it was called the "Ames Monument," having been built to the memory of Oakes Ames, the first president of the Union Pacific R. R. The solitude of the spot where the cairn stands may be judged by the fact that a large wolf slunk away from the track and shambled out of sight among the sage and rocks just before we reached it. But, doubtless, the angels look down with approval on the work of those who loved their leader well enough to build that fitting tribute, gathered from the wilds through which he first beat a permanent highway.

At Cheyenne, I found many intelligent and earnest women, but the state of affairs sometimes before encountered, where the pastors of the churches had not yet learned that upon practice and faith, and not upon theory and form, rests the salvation of human souls, met me at the outset. With the exception of the pastor of the M. E. Church, who was absent on my arrival, and possibly one or more whom I did not meet, the ministers of the city were standing as stumbling blocks in the way of temperance work. As a consequence of their refusing to act with the W. C. T. U., the women were much embarrassed, which necessitated my exposing myself in the chilling air late at night in a search, with the local president, for a minister who considered the preservation of the human body—the "temple of God"—from defilement, a part of Christianity. The result was a severe cold, which turned the pleasure of meeting the large audience that greeted me in the M. E. Church on the second evening after my arrival into a stern duty, discharged only by force of will.

On Sunday afternoon, I visited the jail in company with members of the Union and found the women prisoners occupying the same department as the men. Two colored girls were the only female inmates at the time, and as they were allowed the liberty of an upper corridor reached by steps close to where we stood, I was about to ascend and request them to join in the service, when the gentlemanly young official in charge checked me in well meant solicitude, and informed me that they were very immoral women; unconsciously ignoring the probability that many of his brothers behind the bars, with whom we were even then conversing, were the same.

So, it appeared that the distinction without a difference between sin in women and sin in men was still standing in the way of an equal equality. Recognizing no such distinction, I invited the women, and found them attentive listeners.

CHAPTER XIV.

Another jaunt of over two hundred miles was to bring me to North Platte, Nebraska, and as the "overland flyer" on which I took passage bowled down the steep declivity from Cheyenne to the Platte River Valley at a rate that caused a constant rocking and swaying of the coaches, I found the speed fully in harmony with my mood as I began to realize that I was at last on the Eastern, instead of the Western, Slope, and that the unbroken wanderings of a year and seven months, with their hardships and pleasures, would soon be over.

The last scene of the panorama of lone brown plains, snow-capped mountains, bunch grass ranches, immense wheat fields, water scenery, deep forests, moss, sand drifts, sage brush and calcined cliffs was swiftly running out, and before I realized the significance of the rapid change in landscape, I saw wide, level plains, straight fences, orderly looking farm houses in cultivated groves, and a general appearance of enterprise and prosperity.

Being obliged to remain at North Platte four days, I made some inquiries concerning the hardships from crop failures in Nebraska, and found that the new settlers in the northwestern counties had been the principal sufferers.

"Those counties are much higher than it is here, and the higher you go, the less rain falls," explained a gentleman with whom I conversed on the subject.

But there were no signs of suffering in the Platte River Valley, which, with the valley of the North Platte, makes up a wide strip of country running the entire length of the state from west to east, and in which crops are very seldom a failure.

Missing Kearney by reason of delay at North Platte, I visited the small towns of Gibbon and Shelton before reaching Grand Island, which is a city of ten thousand inhabitants. There, Mrs. R. T. W. Pierce, sister of Judge Samuel Wood, who was brutally murdered in Kansas, took me over the entire city, which was in the bustle of preparation for the holidays and presented a very Eastern appearance.

Clark's, Silver Creek, Columbus, Schuyler and North Bend completed the list of stopping points before reaching Fremont, the home of Mrs. M. A. Hitchcock, president of the Nebraska W. C. T. U., and also the location of a fine W. C. T. U. temple, erected by contributions from different parts of the state.

Notwithstanding Nebraska's large foreign population, I nowhere met with the obtuseness often encountered in town to town journeying, but found a remarkable degree of intelligence among the women throughout the state. The W. C. T. U., through its president, Mrs. Hitchcock, was the first to hear and heed the cry of want from the sufferers in the dry districts, and through its efforts, in first calling on the white-ribboners of the nation for aid, and then receiving and distributing the supplies, relief was given.

The moral part of the population of the state had not yet recovered from its defeat by the forces of evil in the campaign that had just passed, however, and in no place was that fact more apparent than in Omaha, the headquarters from which had emanated the covert ways and vile schemes that had made the defeat possible. There, the more timid of the defeated, instead of floating their banners from the "topmost roofs" and thus insuring recognition, had, apparently, fallen into the error of conciliating an unworthy foe, and were maintaining a self-imposed obscurity.

Communication having been had with the superintendent of the Department of Social Purity of the State Union, who resided in Omaha, I went to her residence on arriving and was pleasantly surprised to find in her Mrs. G. W. Clark, formerly of Cleveland, O., and still possessing the "never surrender" spirit of the Crusade. Having charge of the "Open Door," an institution for unfortunate women, established by the Buckingham W. C. T. U., of Omaha, but supported largely by the locals throughout the state, she was doing a great work in her department; and wherever the "spirit of fear" had not taken possession, there seemed to be no obstacle in the way of advancement.

The holidays had come and gone before I reached Omaha, but the severe winter weather that had come with them gave promise of remaining, and as I journeyed over the Northwestern R. R. to Chicago, I realized that the season for sight-seeing was past. After remaining two days in the latter city, I started on the last stage of journeyings amounting to over nine thousand miles, reaching Cleveland on January 12th, 1892, a year and over eight months from the time of going out.

The impossibility of mentioning by name the many pastors of churches who gave willing assistance in many ways, and the great number of women both in and out of the white ribbon army who aided my work by various acts of kindness, which are all garnered in my memory, is too apparent for explanation to be necessary; but to the following, I wish herein to express my fullest gratitude for special favors :

Mr. Tom D. Campbell, of Cleveland, O., District Passenger Agent of the Northern Pacific R. R., with whom fairness and courtesy are evidently a part of business, and whose thoroughness in the discharge of the duties of his office has saved me much trouble.

The Officers and Agents of the Union Pacific R. R., who willingly granted favors, and kindly imparted helpful information.

Rev. John N. Denison, formerly of Port Townsend, Wash., but now of Portland, Ore., for letters of introduction and assistance in making appointments.

Captain Morgan, of Port Townsend, Wash.

The Officers of the Northwestern R. R.

Mrs. N. E. De Spain, of Pendleton, Ore., whose rare concern for my comfort was like the "shadow of a great rock in a weary land."

Rev. O. C. Billings, Oxford, Idaho.

Dr. Orpha D. Baldwin, E. Portland, Ore., who received and forwarded my correspondence, reaching me promptly and accurately with mail matters in all the highways and byways, thus saving me much perplexity.

Mrs. Noah Cornutt, Riddle's, Ore., the latchstring of whose home was always on the outside.

In conclusion I will say that one of the greatest needs of the New Northwest is such settlers as wish to make homes. It has no need for speculators—it has enough. The professions, also, are overrun ; but those who wish to make homes, which are the great need of the American nation, need not fear to go out and seek them ; for the opportunities are numberless. Two things are always to be considered in selecting a home, and those are, water and fuel. West of the Cascade Mountains, there is no lack of either, and there are yet many, many thousands of acres unsurveyed by the Government, and, consequently, not yet on the market. Land near either the railroad or water transportation is much preferable to any other, as isolation from society and distance to markets must be considered.

THE END.

www.ingramcontent.com/pod-product-compliance
Lightning Source LLC
Chambersburg PA
CBHW020252170426
43202CB00008B/337